*The*Naked*Church*

Exposing your Community to the Church

Authors:
Julian Richards
Daniel Boucher
Iestyn Davies
Rob James
Elfed Godding

Edited by
Alison Walley

The Naked Church

Exposing your Community to the Church

ISBN No : 0-9546989-1-6

Published by:
Shedhead Productions
Antioch Centre
Copperworks Road
Llanelli
SA15 2NE

Printed in Great Britain by:
J.D.Lewis & Sons Ltd
Gwasg Gomer
Llandysul
Ceredigion
SA44 4QL

Contents

Foreword

In the late eighties I was invited to deliver a series of local church and community outreach seminars on behalf of Mission Wales. I took the decision to resist the temptation to reach for familiar notes and materials but instead took a fresh look at the subject. It was decision that changed my ministry focus to this very day.

The combination of a message and actions creates authenticity for the church in the eyes of the community. It builds bridges, breaks down barriers and fleshes out the message of God's love in ways that can be felt, touched and tangibly observed.

We live in a different world these days - some have likened it to a tsunami of change. There is a poverty of trust and integrity. Hype, spin and the sales pitch creates resistance, mistrust and suspicion in the hearts of most people. Churches that are purely message-driven run the risk of driving away the very people they're seeking to attract. A church that combines a clear message with compassionate actions not only, in my view, is an obedient and balanced church, but a strategic and effective church.

Issues such as social justice, community regeneration, volunteerism and movements for change are at the heart of today's society. Engagement in politics is decreasing but Band Aid, Comic Relief and the voluntary sector in general, are connecting with people's concern and hunger to make a difference and live with a purpose.

A church that engages in community services and social action is a church in step with the mood of society. It is a church that demonstrates authenticity and purpose to the world. It is a church that brings credibility to its life-changing message and moves with compassion.

I am therefore delighted to present this latest Gweini publication, '*The Naked Church*'. I pray you will be inspired, challenged and informed as you read. I pray this book will move you to act and to be a part of a great movement of change that once again will cause the church to take its place and effectively demonstrate that it truly is the salt of the earth and the light of the world.

Julian Richards
Director of Gweini

PART 1
IN THE WORLD

by Julian Richards

Chapter 1: The Challenge

The challenge of engagement

During the 1960s the remote island of Tristan da Cunha became uninhabitable due to a volcanic eruption. The British Navy rescued the islanders and brought many of them back to mainland Britain. The last significant contact with the real world that the islanders had had was during the Victorian period. They had lived in isolation for so long that when the navy arrived, they still spoke with a Victorian-Cockney accent, and the women wore Victorian style dresses down to their ankles.

The rescue mission brought them back to the mainland, with its fast cars, mini skirts, Beatle-mania and a changed world. The culture shock was so great that many of the islanders hired boats and went back to Tristan because they would rather withdraw to the familiarity of their devastated homeland than face the challenges and changes of living in an unfamiliar world. I am sure many of us in the church identify with the feeling of the Tristan islanders; how many times have we retreated into the safety of our fellowships and church programmes rather than embrace the pain and challenges of learning to work, serve and relate into a new culture and world?

The Church is the Body of Christ. Expressing that fact by working out the implication of it could be said to be one of the church's greatest challenges. There has always been temptation for the people of God to remove themselves from this world into a safe place of isolation. The motives for this are often very honourable and pure but the results can be devastating for communities and society at large.

One of the reasons for withdrawal from the real world can be a misapplication of the scripture "Come out from them and be separate" (2 Cor. 6:17). This is a common verse used to justify not getting involved. It would be helpful to remind ourselves that Jesus said that we are in the world but not a part of it (John 17: 16). He also said, "Go into all the world and preach the good news." (Mark 16:15). Scripture instructs us to separate ourselves from the values and the sin of the world but not its culture and people.

Another scripture that has been sincerely used in a wrong way is "Avoid every kind of evil" (1 Thess. 5:22). On the surface of things, this verse appears to tell us to keep away from engaging in our world and communities because there appears so much out there that would be incompatible with our faith. But when one looks at this verse in the context of what Paul is saying, he is not talking about evil in the world, but testing prophecy and the need to avoid what does not prove to be genuine. It is quite impossible to avoid every kind of evil if you really want to take the salt and light of God beyond the boundary of a church meeting. Not even Jesus himself when he was on earth avoided every appearance of evil. He was accused of being a friend of tax collectors and sinners, and even of being a drunkard and a glutton.

If we are to engage with our communities, there may be some siege mentality and theology that we may have to revisit. The church can sometimes be like a fortified castle with a drawbridge up and the only time it comes down is when we raid our communities with evangelistic crusades, which usually take place around summer, Easter or Christmas. We are invisible and absent from our communities virtually all year round until we come at them over the hill with a message of 'repent and believe', usually without warning, and find ourselves (not surprisingly) unwelcome. The church often withdraws from its contact with the world in order to preserve purity, values and religious conviction. Many are afraid that contact with the world will contaminate the church and compromise their faith. I believe the preservation and withdrawal mindset hamstrings our evangelism and hides our light. In playing it safe, so many opportunities are lost.

The world feels the church is irrelevant to its everyday life. One cannot blame people for feeling this way when the church has so little to do with the felt needs and issues that people face in their daily routine. Most people see church as a Sunday meeting that they have no intention of going to. What if church was seen as a community of God's people who were actively involved in helping? Helping by improving and changing the local community, practically enhancing the quality of everyday life and meeting people at their point of need with real and tangible solutions.

What if church was not seen as a meeting, but a group of people who had a clear faith in Jesus, who were so involved with making a difference in practical ways that the withdrawal of that faith group would be a noticeable loss for the community? Imagine a church where the power of being the Body of Christ was so felt in the world, that people felt and identified with church even before they attended any kind of meeting.

A strange thing can happen to church Christians after a few years of church attendance; it is called 'redemption and lift'. We get redeemed and lifted out of all significant relationships that may not be Christian. So much time is spent within the community of faith and so little time in the community outside of church that the ability to relate to the unchurched world is lost. So many people have said to me "I feel awkward with non-Christians, I have nothing in common with them, I do not know what to say."

It is as if the church has lost the ability to love outside of the circle of faith. The story of the Good Samaritan and crossing over the road, to heal a wound, meet a felt need and love one's neighbour is all about the ability to express love. When the church withdraws from the world into the security of its meetings and fellowship times, it soon discovers it can only relate to the world through cold contact evangelism. The church gets caught between a rock and a hard place. The commission to preach the Gospel compels the church to 'go out', but she has no bridges into the community to travel over, no friends to persuade and no mechanism for demonstrating love that gives a context to the message. The church has no means by which she as the messenger can be received so that the message may be heard.

When this happens, we tend to become insular and plough most of our resources into maintaining meetings. This can easily lead to a 'building' or 'sanctuary' mentality whereby we begin to value our building more than those whom Christ came to save and serve. Here are some of the ways these mentalities can hinder what God wants to do in and through us:

- The building becomes a holy place dedicated for worship to God only.
- The decor and furnishing support the main function of worship and religious gathering, thereby restricting building use.
- Use of the building for anything other than worship and religious meetings is seen as inappropriate.
- All that takes place within the building becomes sanitised, which is restrictive when dealing with the community.
- The goal of the church is to fill the building on a Sunday, rather than fill the community with salt and light.
- Disunity quickly develops within the church as members disagree as to what are or aren't

acceptable activities and events within the building.

- Our language concerning church communicates to the unchurched a false picture as to what church is and can hinder our evangelistic efforts.

The New Testament clearly shows us that the church is not a building; rather it is the Body of Christ, the family of God. Despite this wonderful truth, the majority of our faith and worship is still expressed within the context of a church service in a building, and the result being that we live as if church is a meeting. We may not believe this theologically, but in practice we often live as if it is.

It is true to say that most of what we do as the people of God is in the context of some kind of meeting. Most of our time is channelled into organised meetings and a significant amount of finance is channelled into maintaining and promoting them. Most of our brilliant speakers, singers, musicians, administrators and leaders are serving the maintenance and success of some kind of meeting, event or programme. The church has a bad case of 'meeting-itus' and many of its members are suffering from meeting fatigue. Seeing church as the meeting is so ingrained in our thinking that we struggle to think creatively of how we could effectively express our faith outside of one. Like the Tristan Islanders, we have withdrawn from expressing our faith in the real world for so long that we have lost the ability to relate, and feel more comfortable when we retreat back to the safety of our meetings.

The challenge of identification

Identification is a key for the church if we are to truly be effective in our endeavour to bring Christ to the world. The invisible God identified with a fallen humanity the moment he clothed himself with flesh and blood, as Romans 8:3 states:

For what the law was powerless to do in that it was weakened by the sinful nature, God did by sending his own Son in the likeness of sinful man to be a sin offering. And so he condemned sin in sinful man...

Paul helps us understand that Jesus took on the likeness of sinful humanity. Even though he knew no sin, he identified with us who did. The church in recent years has been seen to be irrelevant to the average person in the street. If the church were not around, who would really miss it, or realise it had gone? It is not that we are not wanted, but we are not perceived to be needed. Identification with the needs, wounds and issues of our community can move the church from irrelevancy to relevancy, from being not wanted to being needed. Identification is when one applies the issues and challenges of others to oneself personally. It is not just recognising some pain or problem, but also choosing to own it and to do something about it.

Why are doctor's surgeries always full? - because doctors recognise sickness not from afar but 'up close and personal' and do something about it! The

Greyhound Bus Company in the USA said, "When you deal in basic needs you're always wanted." This is a lesson that Jesus demonstrated and the church would do well to learn and copy. The church that ministers to the identifiable needs of its community immediately becomes relevant, needed and wanted. Churches that identify with poverty, crime, lack of child and youth provision, unemployment, health issues and social exclusion within their communities in such a way that they seek to do something about it will soon become centres of community, not alienated from it.

Serving those who are unchurched at their point of felt need will build bridges for the church and help her to once again take her place in community and city life. Market researchers have identified the fact that the new style of consumer looks for authenticity in a product as a high priority before they commit to a purchase. The brand name means very little these days if it does not demonstrate authenticity. The world is looking for this quality in the church before it will believe or accept her. The language of authenticity for the new generation is not words but actions.

Actions speak loudly to the postmodern world. This is why the present generation has more volunteerism than any other. It is also interesting to consider that the voluntary sector is so large now that it is known as the 'third sector' next to government and industry. Social action is the recognisable language of the day that communicates, 'You are the genuine article.' If the church wants to make an impact on this generation, it has to speak today's language through actions and social action.

Engagement and identification, meeting felt needs and serving our communities are the ways back to taking our place as salt and light, and will build a bridge enabling us to cross over so we can love our neighbour. These ways are the road to relevance, communicating that we are genuine and can be trusted because we care. Then the world will see we care because God cares. They are the means by which the messenger is received so that the message of the Gospel may be heard and understood from the context of a serving community, a body in the world, the Church of Jesus Christ.

It is not social action that saves people because indeed it does not - repentance and faith that comes through receiving the message of the Gospel brings salvation. The point is that if we want people to listen to the message, the authenticity and relevance of the messenger is vital.

The challenge of expressing our salt and light

The Church is on the earth to be salt. Salt in the first-century world was of great worth and usefulness. Often workers would be paid in salt, which is where we get the word 'salary' from and the phrase 'worth their salt'. Salt has many effective properties that are worth considering in the light of Jesus' statement that we are the salt of the earth, and therefore should function like salt.

Salt has preserving qualities. It was used to smother onto meat before the days of refrigeration in order to stop decay setting in. Likewise, the church also has a moral decay-preventing power within her, as she comes into contact with the world and society that she is placed into.

Salt creates a thirst and a desire for water. The church also has the power to create a thirst and desire for Christ and the true living water of the Holy Spirit to meet the deepest need of the human heart. As the church rubs shoulders with those who are unchurched, as our lives are observed and the quality of our relationships are seen, a desire for and interest in spiritual things can quickly develop in people's hearts.

Salt also has a healing property that, if placed on a wound, an infection may be prevented and recovery speeded. As the body of Christ engages in our broken and wounded community, with all its pain and relational breakdown, God can speed up and supply a healing and restoration to the wounds and lives of many people.

The challenge of course is to get the church out of the container of our meetings, out of our church building mindsets, and into the meat and wounds of the world and society in which we live.

Jesus said we are the light of the world (Matt. 5: 14-15). Light is for shining in dark places and being placed where people can see the light. Sometimes as church we do not realise how much light we have to give because it is mostly shone where a lot of light already shines. This is like taking a lit candle into a room where a 100-watt light is already shining. It does not make much of a difference.

If most of our time, service, finance and resources are channelled and kept in the environment where there is already a lot of light (church in a building or meetings), the light we have is not noticed. Jesus said, "Let your light shine before men so they can see...", thus indicating he wants our light to be seen. The next part of the verse is key in making our light visible and Jesus continues, "That they might see your good deeds." We need to be doing good works in a place where the light can get out and be seen, where those who do not know Christ can see it.

So we see that as the church serves in its locality with good deeds, its light is seen. As the church becomes a good neighbour to wounded humanity, light shines from her to the world. As we cross over, engage and become a body in the world as Christ has, his light shines out, is therefore seen, and then (dare I say), recognised. When Christ's light is seen through our good works, the result is that those who observe glorify God: "let your light shine before men, that they may see your good deeds and praise your Father in heaven."

The other matter to note from this passage is that our good works are to be a vehicle for the Holy Spirit to reveal Christ's light and glory to men and women, boys and girls. So we observe that as the church, the Body of Christ, engages in the world and fleshes out the invisible Christ with its saltiness and good acts, Christ's glory and light is seen and beheld again and again until he returns.

I believe it is necessary for the church to engage in its community by serving if it wishes to be relevant and effective in reaching out to the unchurched. Nobody drives a twenty-ton truck over a two-centimetre plywood bridge. The message of the Gospel is a message of challenge and hope. Serving the community builds a bridge strong enough for the message to cross over. However it is not just about being relevant as church, or being evangelistically effective, or building bridges. It is about encompassing and living a life of love that pleases God and expresses his kindness to all.

For the past eleven years I have had the privilege of leading Cornerstone Church into serving the community in Swansea. We receive as many as 1,400 visits a month to our church centre that serves in an area of severe social exclusion. Yes, the church is growing. Yes, people from the community are regularly turning to Christ. Yes, we have great influence and acceptance within the community and city, and yes - it works!

But even if nobody became a Christian though our social action, we would still do it. Why? Because God cares, and it pleases him when we reach and touch the pain of those he has created. It pleases him when we cross over and love our neighbour.

PART 2
DEMONSTRATING CHRIST'S COMPASSION

by Rob James

Chapter 2: Linden Church

Patience is a Christian virtue and this is especially so when thinking about mission. Jesus made that abundantly clear in the parable of the sower. As he draws to a conclusion Luke tells us that the good soil "represents honest, good-hearted people who hear God's message, cling to it and steadily produce a harvest". (Luke 8:15, New Living Translation).

Jesus knew ministry would be difficult. He was well aware of the disappointments and setbacks that plague our efforts to serve him. He did not get an easy ride and he wanted all those who followed him to know that they wouldn't get one either. He also knew that we can only be spiritually productive if we are willing to persevere and remain steadfast whatever the difficulties.

Luke uses the Greek word *hupomone*. "*Hupomone,*" writes William Barclay, "does not describe the patience that sits down with folded hands and bowed head and simply passively submits to the tide of events; *hupomone* describes the spirit of courage and conquest which begets gallantry and transmutes even suffering into glory."

Linden Church, based in the west of Swansea, has discovered the importance of patient endurance. Linden has a clear vision that God expects it to be involved in its local community. Church Finance Officer Janet Hurst explains, "Our motive for working in the community is to do as Jesus said and help those in need, especially those who can't help themselves. If people see Jesus in us, and in what we do, that's good, but it's not a condition for us to work with them. One of our prime purposes is to do as Jesus would do and love them for who they are."

This biblical vision gave birth to the Connected Project and the Red Café. In so doing it has taught the church that given patience it is possible to discover that God is still willing to do more than we could ever expect or even imagine.

In Spring 2000 the church bought an old guesthouse in Southend, a part of Mumbles with many bars and nightclubs. Members had long wanted to provide safe, alternative facilities for young teenagers in Mumbles. When a suitable property became available they agreed to take out a mortgage to buy it with a view to turning it into a youth café.

Work duly started on the building but then they reached an impasse. An extra £15,000 was needed to complete the refurbishment but the church simply did not have the money. Taking encouragement from the Scriptures the church met for prayer and discussion and ultimately decided to step out in faith and give the go-ahead for the work "trusting funding would come through".

And as always the Lord proved that he is a God of surprises. He did not provide them with the money but with an even greater challenge. As Janet explains, "The very next day the church office was contacted and asked if it was interested in buying the property next door as well! Over a matter of days Linden went from needing £15,000 to needing £120,000."

When the apostle Paul wanted to encourage the believers in Rome he cited the example of Abraham. "When God promised Abraham that he would become the father of many nations Abraham believed him. God had also said 'Your descendants will be as numerous as the stars,' even though such a promise seemed utterly impossible. And Abraham's faith did not weaken even though he knew that he was too old to be a father at the age of one hundred and that Sarah his wife had never been able to have children. Abraham never wavered in believing God's promise. In fact his faith grew stronger and in this he brought glory to God." (Rom. 4:18-20) But of course it took time, commitment - and patient endurance, as Linden has discovered too.

To begin with it took great faith, based on the conviction that God had spoken and the church needed to act on that, whatever the cost. Lots more prayer and discussion took place and then an understanding bank provided a 100% mortgage. Linden church now 'owned' two adjacent properties on the sea front, but as any householder knows, that's simply where the journey begins.

Not surprisingly, the need for funding began to focus their minds. The church had briefly flirted with European Fund applications earlier that spring but they had been put to one side (they were "too difficult" and "too gobbledegook"). Janet Hurst now felt it was time to take funding possibilities seriously. "I decided to have a go at the forms again myself," she explains, "although it was with great trepidation. We made an application to the European Regional Development Fund (ERDF) for help towards the cost of the refurbishment and the setting up of the café."

And just as God tested Abraham he tested Linden. "We received a long letter with many, many questions to answer," Janet says. "I'd downloaded reams from the Internet when completing the form and again had to wade through the terminology. I felt as if I'd written a thesis as my reply. Everything is governed by rules and regulations - including one I had missed or probably misunderstood - that said that ERDF money could not be used for things that were more than 50% complete. The purchase was complete in deed even if paid for by a mortgage that was nowhere near 50% paid off!"

With a wry smile she continues, "After a lot of hassle the application was turned down. But boy, had we learned a lot. It almost felt like a game! I did wonder why it had not been turned down immediately

- but then as I'd never had any higher education I suppose I would never have had the chance to write such a dissertation if we had not done this."

It was not all doom and gloom however. The Connected Project had also put its Red Café forward to be part of a European Partnership Project entitled Swansea Youth Activities. This was accepted and this entitled them to an exciting source of funding from the European Social Fund.

Like all Christian ventures the Red Café could not operate without the help of committed volunteers, to man the café as well as engage in all sorts of activities behind the scenes (such as decorating and maintenance). Under the terms of the ESF the project was able to place a value on their hours and receive a percentage of the calculated monetary value of all this (see Chapter 9). This was tremendously encouraging because it meant that people who couldn't afford to contribute cash could give time and earn money for the project at the same time.

Not surprisingly, given this level of prayer and personal commitment, the project proved to be a great success. Opening three nights a week and in school holidays Red Café attracts a steady number of youngsters. It provides "a place to chill" as well as offering a range of helpful facilities such as alternative education in sound engineering, music, green issues and IT.

And so, emboldened by the blessing and chastened by their mistakes the project administrators felt they ought to try for larger funding again. "When it became inevitable (as we always hoped it would) that the café needed to expand into next door, it was another member, Helen, who was prepared to spend days and long sleepless nights on the new application," Janet explains. "We had gained in confidence, helped and encouraged by the many others we were now beginning to network with. Through their experience, she and others involved in funding applications had at last learned some of this strange new language. We decided to make an application to the Welsh Assembly's Community Facilities and Activities Programme because that seemed one of the simplest on offer, and there was also the chance that they would fund it one hundred per cent."

Patience was needed yet again. There were delays and no news, and because of this the decision was taken to apply for ERDF again. The team knew that compared to some costly bids the Connected Project application was quite small, but it still had to stand on its merits. Helen nervously presented the application to the subgroup of the Swansea funding panel that vets local European bids and thankfully they judged that there appeared to be a market for what the project was seeking to do. The bid was passed on with their recommendation and all involved began to pray for the 41% match funding.

Janet continues the story. "One couple were so serious about this that they had been fasting from alcohol since the spring. They really wanted that wall to come down and they were beginning to wonder how long they would have to continue. And then we had a little encouragement because the ERDF telephoned us with some questions. We realised at that moment that it might still go through.

"After lots of frantic phone calls and advice we felt we should ask the Welsh Assembly if there was any news about their fund and if they would match fund the European bid instead of Linden. ERDF was approved - and they did. It was a long time coming but it had come at last. The shrieks of delight emanating from volunteers and workers in Red Café must have been heard in County Hall.

"We were so excited when we heard about it. It means that some of our own future funds can now be channelled elsewhere - perhaps even pay off some of our mortgage. But there is also the question of those other issues raised in the area survey we had done some time earlier. What about a West Cross Forum to coordinate local community work? What about the land alongside our premises? What about bringing community facilities into our locality? What about....?"

Looking back, with the extension to the café half complete and the dream almost a reality, Janet says that all concerned are convinced that "it was definitely worth the hassle".

"It was frustrating," she admits, "and it was hard going at times. But we've learned a lot too, especially the importance of communication, record-keeping and good business practice. And we've proved that it's possible for even a small voluntary group like ours to be successful in a European bid."

And Janet has this advice for anyone contemplating a similar step of faith. "Some groups, especially churches, feel discriminated against when they're asked lots of questions, but they need to remember that it is public money and it must be properly accounted for. As we've got to know people we've discovered that they really are trying to help us in every way and make us think carefully about our bid to ensure that it stands the best chance. We never realised how much work the record keeping would be either and with hindsight we are glad now that we were turned down the first time because it allowed us to learn more and more as we kept knocking on doors.

"It's a bit like having a baby. You suddenly realise that there's a lot more hard work than you realised at first, but with this there are fixed rules and regulations outside your control too. We are still struggling with all the documentation but at long last we are beginning to see the need and the reasoning behind a lot of it. Not all of it, of course, but then things have to cover a wide area of use and we're learning that some of our questions won't be able to be answered yet. It's a bit like faith really and so we can go with that!"

Janet has practical suggestions for any church group or Christian organisation that wants to demonstrate God's love in their communities. "Don't give up. Get financial systems into place, research your area, ask questions, get lots of advice and make sure that you have people that are willing and equipped to be business-like and prepared for a lot of hard work. You will definitely need someone who is willing to spend at least 40 hours a week on the planning and application process and this could mean becoming an employer.

"We have recently taken on our third full-time employee and we also have ten others who work part-time too. They are not all involved directly with the Connected Project but we are applying the lessons we have learned there too. European funding is there until 2006 but there are lots of other funds too. Take advice, go on training days, talk and network. The most important thing of course is prayer, but whatever you decide DON'T GIVE UP".

It's been well said that our God is a missionary God. Abraham was called to leave his people and his country because God wanted to make him a blessing for every nation on earth. Tragically Israel kept forgetting the universal scope of God's promise. The church does the same all too often too. But the God who sent his Son and who has given us his Spirit has also promised that we need not worry about the resources. All he asks for is commitment, a willingness to obey His voice and the kind of faith that is spelled RISK.

The apostle Paul gave this advice to the church: "Don't get tired of doing good. Don't get discouraged and give up, for we will reap a harvest of blessing at the appropriate time." (Gal. 6:9, NLT) By remaining steadfast Linden church is reaping that blessing, but better still, the young people of Mumbles are clearly enjoying the fruits.

Chapter 3: Thornhill Church

Words fascinate me. Take the word 'opportunity'. Who would ever have guessed that it derives from a Latin word that was used originally of wind driving towards the harbour? We can learn a lot by reflecting on the words used in the Greek New Testament too.

Take the word *kairos*. It means time but it also means much more than that. It signifies "the right moment", a critical time, one which demands a decision. When used positively it implies advantage; when used negatively it highlights danger. *Kairos* could also mean the right spot or a suitable place. There are those who would argue that the last few years have been a *kairos* time for Thornhill Church, Cardiff, as God has shown the members what it means to be in the right place at the right time.

Thornhill is on the north of Cardiff. It did not exist 20 years ago but recent housing developments have resulted in a community of nearly 3,000 homes. The church began some 19 years ago when a small group of Christians moved into the area and began to meet together. Over the years it has developed into a sizeable congregation that meets and ministers through a new purpose-built church centre.

Community Pastor Alex Wilson explains. "The community had been developing, but the thing that was missing was a sense of community. A vision grew for a building that was at the very centre of the community and we persuaded the local council that we could be in partnership with the local community; not only a church but a centre that could be used in the local community. We set about working out how we should do this. How would the community benefit from such a building as this?

"The church centre is now possibly at the heart of that development. Five years ago we managed to build this place with some 41 people from the church. We have a coffee shop that is open six days a week. We have a nursery that has a waiting list. We have events for senior citizens. Meeting Points is a place where folks can come and meet. There are a number of youth activities and we have very close ties with the local supermarket - they come here to hold seminars. The local Health Centre holds regular antenatal classes and recently two of our members became part of that group and began a new work called First Time Mums."

"The building was largely funded by the church, with some supporting grants from the local council and a few charities. The building design was in keeping with the other buildings in the district centre and looks no different to any other modern community centre. It is open seven days a week for about 13 hours a day and over 2,000 people use it every week. The success of the Nursery and the Coffee Shop is an example of best practice in community development. The community vision has been clearly incredibly successful and the community is already outstripping the facilities."

Thornhill Church Centre is now entering a new and potentially very exciting stage in its very short history. In a draft brief prepared in 2002 for the local authority the church leadership said, "The local councillors have seen the potential of a public/private partnership with the centre, developing the remainder of the site in a 'win-win way' providing a Council Library for North Cardiff and significantly increasing the community facilities in Thornhill and Llanishen."

Intriguingly, the Council made the initial approach, emphasising the fact that "due to a lack of resources for capital projects they were unlikely to be able to realise their interests in Thornhill without such a partnership agreement."

Consequently the Trustees of the project have conducted an extensive audit of community needs and researched modern community development interventions geared to the building of 'social capital in communities'. The resulting principles included in the brief are: social inclusion; employment; education; training; targeting under fives, youth, the elderly, lower social classes, the socially excluded; creating and enhancing social networks; health promotion.

The proposed schedule of rooms would include such facilities as a small multi-gym, a small sanctuary for prayer and meditation and a patio and landscaped area to maximise the natural amenities of the site.

Writing in *Leadership Today* Gordon MacDonald said,

> *"The modern Christianity I know is too wordy. We talk about what we should do and lash ourselves for what we're not doing (or why we think we're doing it). And then when it's all over we talk about what we did and what significance we think it had. Oh, and we talk an awful lot about what 'the world' is or shouldn't be doing. I fear I am a major donor to this palaver.*
>
> *"Much of this talking I fear, seems to be bent on convincing ourselves that we (or our organisations) are significant and that what we are doing deserves other people's praise or, alternatively, their financial gifts. As I have said, some of our talk seems targeted on those who have pursued other ways than ours. If we can highlight how bad, how different, how misguided they are, then we can justify what we are doing. And that makes us feel better."*

Thankfully Thornhill Church escapes such censures, for it has discovered what it means to be salt and light in its needy (and obviously appreciative) community. And it's clearly not been done without a great deal of prayer and discussion among the leadership and the membership. The prospect of an extended ministry and bigger facilities are exciting but they also raise fundamental issues that the church has had to address.

Recognising the Lordship of Jesus over his church, Thornhill has carefully sought to ensure that they have never felt rushed or pushed by the council. God's will has been paramount and the leadership has seen that evidenced in many ways. There has been a sincere desire to address hard questions in a way that will allow the church to move forward in a united manner. In seeking to encourage the membership to believe that the Lord is at work through the local council's approach the leadership explains, "Some had been praying for the possibility of extended facilities before the councillors approached us."

In addition to the pressure for extra space the church has also received encouragement from God's word. They have also been able to point to the many confirmations that God has been blessing their ministry principles.

The church has also worked hard to ensure that it did not allow its building programme to become a primary goal. Thornhill believes that the main purpose of the church is to worship and to witness. There is a deep conviction that they can witness to the Lord in their worship and in their witness within the community. The vision of Thornhill has always been, and continues to be, the extension of God's Kingdom in individual lives, families and in the wider community. "The intention is not to build buildings but to build the Kingdom of God. The intention is ministry not buildings."

Like many growing churches Thornhill has a manpower problem, but the leadership does not believe this should act as a brake on growth. The leaders readily admit that there is an increasing problem in obtaining sufficient workers for all the current ministries but they are committed to extending the current facilities. Several arguments have been offered in support of this.

"We would be investing in the future and would not necessarily need to do everything from the start. The church is growing slowly but steadily, and this will mean a growing number of ministers. We can take encouragement from what happened with phase 1. As the work has grown God has always provided what we needed, as we have prayed according to our needs. Also the evidence is that people respond to vision and are keen to be part of God's Kingdom work.

"We believe that God always wants our faith to grow. We have seen God call us to great steps of faith in the past and we are sure that he will continue to do so. It is probable that new and extended ministry would be achieved via paid staff. As a church we have already grown from one administrator to 22 paid staff (part time and full time, pastoral and centre ministries). The funding plan that is being developed assumes a significant increase again in staffing. This would mean that church members could carry out their ministry according to their gift either on a volunteer basis or on a paid basis."

Thornhill church is growing and impacting its community because it is taking God and the issues seriously. The leadership is aware of the possibilities of church planting and would be supportive of those wishing to begin a church in another place, but they are also aware that they have a primary responsibility to Thornhill. "To what degree have we begun to penetrate our current catchment? The reality is about 0.1%! There is probably huge potential yet to 'invade Satan's turf'. However we must make any long-term investments prudently. We should be aware of over stretching the church too far into the future. One of the advantages of developing a church like we are envisioning is that we will be building young people and 'bible school' students to go out into other ministry, maybe church planting all over the world. In that sense we are strategically investing in the future of the church universally."

The Indian mystic Sadhu Sundar Singh once said, "Salt crystals cannot give flavour to food unless they dissolve. If we dissolve salt in a pot it disappears but it does not cease to exist. Indeed it can then give flavour to thousands of grains of rice."

Thornhill Church is taking this incarnational principle seriously. The concept behind the centre is not as an alternative but in addition to church members being salt and light in their secular environments. The idea is that Thornhill Centre is like a 'market place' where thousands of people gather. In that market place the Christian staff and volunteers will then have excellent opportunities to minister the love of Christ to them and bring the Kingdom of God close to them, especially those who are disadvantaged.

Alex Wilson is very up-beat. "The future for us is exciting. The partnership with the local authority has been so successful and very much a part of what we at Thornhill would like to do at the very heart of the community - to be bridge-building in our community, to be reaching out to our community - but also to be involved in the life of our community with no hidden agenda. We want to ask quite simply, 'What can we do for you that will be of benefit to you?'"

The Roman poet Horace meant something quite different but he put it well. "Carpe diem - Seize the day." Thankfully Thornhill church is, and God is getting the glory in Cardiff.

Chapter 4: Cornerstone

I would guess that when the apostle Paul told the church at Corinth that their lives were to be letters read by all men he little dreamed that would happen in a sorting office. But that's just what's happened in Swansea.

Cornerstone Church was pioneered 11 years ago when nine people met in the front room of Julian and Sarah Richards' house. Eleven years later that small house group has evolved into a thriving congregation of approximately 160 people with 12 paid members of staff.

Unusually, the church's growth has come primarily through people coming to faith, and this is a remarkable achievement given the well-documented background of decline and decay in contemporary Wales. And it's not difficult to understand why. The church was founded on the principle of building a community of people that would attract the lost, and at the heart of that was a desire to serve those who lived around it. This vision has been infinitely more than a pipe dream because the 12 members of staff, with the help of many other volunteers, deliver multiple projects and services to the local community, attracting some 1,400 visits a month.

In 1997 the church purchased and refurbished a former GPO sorting office which has been renamed The Cornerstone Church Centre. The centre operates as a base for the worshipping and serving community, and in 2000, thanks to an EU grant, the church was able to respond to the growing demand for community services by completing a £100,000 annexe.

It is said that Saint Francis of Assisi encouraged his followers to preach the gospel, using words if really necessary. He would be delighted with Cornerstone. The church has embraced a holistic concept of mission that stresses the needs of the whole man, and has been both adventurous and industrious in seeking to put those principles into practice.

Pastor Julian Richards, for example, models this missionary ideal. He is currently chairman of a local community development trust and chaplain to the city's mayor. He represents faith groups on the Key Partners' Alliance Committee and on the Welsh Council for Voluntary Action Board (an umbrella organisation that is constitutionally linked to the Welsh Assembly to inform and represent the concerns of Welsh civil society to the National Assembly).

Some of Cornerstone's activities fit well within traditional models of mission within Wales. For example once a week over 200 children are bussed in from the local estates and taken to the Elim Church in Swansea. This inter-church programme consists of an hour's mix of interactive fun, games, songs, quizzes and Bible stories. Cornerstone places great emphasis on the need to reach children on an individual basis however, and as a consequence of this every child is visited in their home by a volunteer each week with a puzzle to complete. This means that over 170 homes in the Swansea area are visited every week.

Lunch clubs continue to be a popular attraction in Daniel James Secondary and Gwyrosydd Junior Schools. The Year Team has also responded to the expressed needs of the local young people by establishing an evening drop-in café at Cornerstone. This aims to offer a safe environment for several dozen middle teens who gather together for informal chats. These activities are yet more examples of Cornerstone's desire to provide high quality provision for local children. The Year Team and the Community Liason Officer have also supported local initiatives set up by other agencies.

Like many other churches Cornerstone also runs a much valued parent and toddler group, known as the Little Rascals. Now in its third year it continues to be a popular and well-run service with around 60 names on the register. The group is staffed by volunteers who provide a variety of activities designed to encourage interaction between parents and young children. These include crafts, educational games, songs and stories. The service also provides support on parenting issues as well as being a point of social contact for parents and children. The Community Liaison Worker carries out home visits to users and has encouraged interested parents to join adult education classes at the centre.

Education ranks highly on Cornerstone's list of priorities. A variety of courses have been offered at the centre in conjunction with Swansea College, offering tuition in courses ranging from First Aid to IT. Cornerstone has also recently established a pilot course for the over 50's in Internet and IT skills in response to research done by the Community Liaison Worker.

Homework Clubs are held too after school, for children struggling with their homework as well as for those who do not have the room or the resources to complete their work at home. This club runs once a week, consists of approximately 30 children, and is also staffed by volunteers.

Cornerstone also has a number of skilled trainers who deliver courses and one-off sessions on such issues as parent-craft, youth and children's work, HIV/AIDS awareness, relationship skills, teamwork and healthy living. These have been delivered to a wide variety of age groups in a number of differing contexts. Most recently, for example, a church-based team has delivered PSE days on drugs and self image for Year 8 and 10 pupils, and boy-girl relationships for year 9 pupils. As a result of this approximately 400 secondary pupils entered the Cornerstone Centre.

There is also a consistent and effective counselling service available for any who wish to take advantage of it. The counsellors are trained and can be accessed directly by all local people and referrals are also taken from the local medical centre. There has been a noticeable increase in this service since the Community Liaison Worker was appointed in May 2001, with more than 71 counselling sessions taking place over the past twelve months. The church is now investigating ways of expanding this service, given the obvious need and the credibility it has attained.

Cornerstone has also initiated a very novel and powerful form of ministry in The Gap, an innovative education package that has won much praise, and continues to be in great demand. The Gap is aimed primarily at young people aged 15 to 16 who are disaffected with the secondary education they have received. Many have long since stopped attending school or have very poor attendance records. Not surprisingly, many of them have poor behaviour records, truant internally, lack social skills and face bleak futures. Some are in danger of exclusion and have been in trouble with the police.

The Gap aims to re-motivate these disaffected young people, and seeks to engage them through a combined programme of indoor and outdoor learning. To further this Cornerstone has pioneered 16 unique courses that reflect in style and content the way teens think and learn today. All these courses have gained proper accreditation, and have earned Cornerstone a name for excellence and delivery. Outdoor pursuits play a key role in this because the team know that such activities offer splendid opportunities for strengthening relationships, building confidence, developing teamwork skills and overcoming fears.

The patriarch Abraham was told he would be both blessed and a blessing to others. Cornerstone is experiencing something of the same relationship with Abraham's God. As it serves its local community, and as it offers practical forms of help to those who live around it, Cornerstone Church is sending out a powerful message from its refurbished post office. It's a message that local people clearly understand and accept as good news. As a result of this Cornerstone is a growing church that is winning an ever-increasing sense of trust and acceptance, both within the local community, and within the city of Swansea. This is quite an achievement at a time when the latest government research points to a marked decline in our willingness to trust one another.

This trust has led to opportunities to provide community leadership and involvement in local and national strategy-making groups and forums. The Gap has been included in an official Welsh Assembly documentation of models of best practice for youth work, and Gap Director Sarah Richards has spoken to several city and UK-wide conferences on youth work, education and youth disaffection.

Cornerstone has demonstrated that to influence the community a church needs to be at the heart of that community. And when it does, it can do more than practise what it preaches, it can also make that message very attractive.

Chapter 5: Antioch

Few churches can claim to touch almost every family in the town, but that's what's happening in Llanelli, and most of the contacts are through Crazy Maisie's.

Crazy Maisie's Fun Station and Nearly New Shop is only one of many expressions of faith sponsored by Antioch Christian Centre in Llanelli, but over the past three years it's had a significant impact on local people.

Antioch Church was started in 1987 by Karen and Mark Lowe and Stuart Watkins. The church grew rapidly, with a willingness to accept people from a variety of backgrounds, particularly those who were socially excluded. As Karen Lowe explains. "Llanelli is a typical post-industrial town that was devastated in the early 80's by the closure of a major steelworks. Over the past few years there has been some major regeneration but there's still a lot further to go."

Antioch clearly thinks it has a crucial role to play in regenerating this devastated society. Indeed it seems to have been doing it from the moment of its birth. "We'd been working with groups of wild youngsters," Karen Lowe continues, "some of whom had been coming to faith, but they really weren't fitting into the chapel culture. We decided to plant a church, which began in the front room of the terraced house Mark and I had rented. We moved into a number of different community halls but at that point we felt that we needed to plant the church again with the values of a passion for the presence of God and a real desire that none should perish."

And God blessed their efforts because they started seeing people coming to faith from all sorts of difficult backgrounds, including prison and addiction. According to Karen it radically changed them as a church for the better. "In the course of this," she says, "we decided we needed a building to facilitate some of the work we were doing in the community, which we had not planned, but had come into being through the people that were being drawn to us. We had been very anti-building but we started looking at pubs, old chapels, and even an undertaker's. In the end we bought 17,000 square feet of semi-dereliction."

Antioch then arose from the ruins of a derelict factory within the old docks area of Llanelli. It provides a base from which the members seek to serve the local community. The present Antioch Centre houses a number of different projects. Antioch is committed to a multi-faceted approach to improving the social and economic life in Llanelli, and this is reflected in the wide range of activities which aim to meet four major areas of need: family support, disadvantaged youth and children, drug and substance abuse, and unemployment.

The church did its homework well before seeking

outside funding. When applying, it was able to argue for example, that "the centre is based in the Glanymor ward and the survey results obtained from the Llanelli Area Forum indicate that the level of social and leisure facilities is poor, with the strongest need being provision for children and young people. The number of children under 18 in the ward on the child protection register is above the Welsh average and there are further demands for community facilities and support for carers and one parent families."

In another grant application to Carmarthenshire County Council they said, "In another area of deprivation there are significant levels of single parent and teenage families, together with a lack of employment opportunities which lead to social and economic marginalisation."

The refurbishment of the building is still in progress but has already achieved in making a base from which the church can serve the whole community. The creation of a drop-in centre for Chooselife's drugs and alcohol intervention activities aims to address the linked problems of alcohol and substance abuse. Thirteen business start-up units and numerous community service units reflect the church's heartfelt concern for the unemployed.

A recording studio is part of the community work of the church too, and offers facilities for local bands to play regularly. Newid also facilitates local voluntary organisations in equipping themselves with PA equipment, provides training in PA and guitar tuition. The studio provides entry-level facilities for the community and places great emphasis on the introduction of techniques and training in the production of good quality CDs.

Aware of its God-given responsibilities because it is located in one of the poorest wards in Wales, Antioch organises various children's and young people's clubs. The activities include teaching, games, outdoor pursuits, social events and vocational skills and aim to provide safe environments where the young people can learn social skills, develop character, personal confidence and abilities.

Antioch also places great emphasis on family support and the church is very much aware that the ward has the highest rate of sexual and physical abuse among children in the whole of Carmarthenshire. A parent and toddler group attracts around 20-30 children on a weekly basis attracted by "an exciting programme of activities and care as well as education for carers who lack ideas and skills. It also sees itself as a natural support group for new parents and carers."

Alongside this volunteers have partnered with local health visitors and Social Services in running a highly successful seven-week course on parenting skills. Health visitors have observed that the relaxed atmosphere at the centre has enhanced the ability of the children to play and the parents to learn. This support group also offers parents a safe place to explore solutions to parenting and other related issues. The programme is ongoing, running every school term. In 2001 funding was secured for a full time Family Support Worker who is responsible for the oversight of the existing programmes but also mandated to develop further initiatives.

Crazy Maisie's is a crucial element in the church's family support programme. Crazy Maisie's Fun Station operates as a business, providing entertainment and employment at the same time. When it was opened in the autumn of 1997 it provided employment for four full-time employees and play facilities for up to 40 children at a time. Parents and children were offered the use of a bouncy castle area, a toddlers' area, a coffee bar and a gift shop within a large room inside the church building.

Mother of 2, Una Brown launched the project with a £15,000 County Council Community Enterprise Award, granted with the aim of creating a high profile, quality daytime fun centre. A nearly-new shop formed part of the initial vision too, selling quality second hand children's clothes and equipment. As Una explained at the time, "We will be selling clothes on an agency basis with a high commission paid to the sellers. We aim to provide viable employment opportunities and pay good wages, as well as generating revenue to complete renovation on the rest of the building. We will also be taking bookings for birthday parties."

Una and the church had clearly done their homework and had established clear aims before embarking on such an ambitious project, as is obvious from her observations at the time. Craisy Maisie's is a business run by the Antioch Centre and was set up with a number of specific aims in mind. Una says, "We wanted to provide a high-quality facility which could be used and enjoyed by the members of the local community both for entertainment and to meet a number of other felt needs in the sectors of the society we represent. We saw the need to address the issue of unemployment locally and we took on a number of staff who underwent various levels of training. We also needed to look at ways of making the centre financially self-sufficient and in the long-term see the business as a way of achieving this.

"We were given significant capital funding from the local authority," she continues, "and had a grant from the European Regional Development Fund to March 2001. We also enjoy the support of many professionals working with local families and we are looking for imaginative ways to see the facility used by able bodied and special needs children and we are working with local charities to this end."

By the end of the year the church was well placed to assess the strengths and weaknesses of the new project. It was clearly making good progress, both in terms of the business generated and the internal development of staffing and management structures. Wisely, the church held a week to evaluate progress with the help of an external management consultant and this culminated in the production of a project plan to take them through the following two years, addressing the major strengths and weaknesses exposed.

Overall the business was clearly successful from the very beginning as Una explained in her report to the church in September 1998. "Our income has increased significantly during this period in all areas but most notably through the birthday party package. We are currently working at full capacity in this area and are looking at ways to increase the number of parties we can accommodate. The shop is gradually increasing in popularity and is seeing steady improvement in sales. During the six-month period April to September it is my estimation that we have seen 4 to 5,000 people, primarily unchurched, using our facilities. This is a major encouragement to us and a real inspiration to pray for the Lord to impact the lives of those who visit."

The original vision of creating jobs has proved challenging and has not been without its disappointments. Initially the project was staffed completely by full-time workers but this had to change. Within a year some 10% of the staffing was voluntary, although this did have the added advantage of involving more church members in the vision. In February 1999 one existing member of staff and two temporary part-time employees were taken on formally under training schemes, with the member of staff completing training to NVQ level 3 and the two others to level 2. By 2001, when Bethan Davies took over as manageress, the project was able to employ three full-time and two part-time staff.

Current manageress Elizabeth Watkins is under no illusions about the size and the financial challenge of her task. As she says, "My priority has been the transforming of a community enterprise reliant on grant funding and a hefty church subsidy into a viable business. We needed to achieve this without our community noticing any change in the quality of the service we offer. It has been a painful transition but we are moving in the right direction. Since October 2002 we have received no cash subsidy from any source. Hidden subsidies still remaining include the fact that we pay no rent to Antioch for the space we occupy, and certain administrative tasks and maintenance are carried out by church employees free of charge."

And Elizabeth's honesty and sense of frustration are evident from her next comments. "Part of the vision was for a job creation project and this is where the main sacrifices have been made to make the business profitable. Full-time staff levels have been cut, with students helping out on Saturdays and holidays, and with early evening parties. We have recently received a LRF grant for the shop, which will release a small wage subsidy at the end of the year. However as an established facility it has proved impossible to attract more grant funding for the Fun Station."

Funding is available for those willing to pursue it diligently. Currently Antioch has approximately 14 projects based at the centre and the church has developed a proper management structure to deal with this. Small management groups ensure good management and also a cohesive approach to grant applications.

Engagement is an essential part of the gospel for the church at Antioch. The members believe that it is important for faith groups who work in the community to actively engage with existing organisations and service providers because that way they can ensure they are working with the community and are not isolated from it.

It's worth remembering that the first church at Antioch was not the result of a major crusade. It was not established by a few outstanding leaders; it was built by a handful of anonymous refugees who had lost everything, whose worlds had been turned upside down, but loved Jesus and showed it. In many ways they were powerless and very ordinary, but they had good news to share and people took note. Thankfully there are disciples in Llanelli today who can also be called "Christians".

Chapter 6: Operation Kindness

Wrexham is not normally associated with good wine but those who understand New Testament Greek will readily appreciate the connection.

Chrestos and *chrestotoes* are usually translated as 'kindness' and 'kind', but the word originally denoted usefulness and therefore anything that was good, suitable and proper. Luke uses the word in this way when he recalls the famous saying of Jesus that people prefer old wine to new because the old is better (*chrestos*) (Luke 5:39).

Christians are supposed to be both useful and kind. In fact the apostle Paul told the church at Corinth that kindness is an essential and unmistakeable characteristic of love (1 Cor. 13). Not surprisingly then, Paul stresses repeatedly that the God we meet in Jesus is incredibly kind. He tells the Christians at Ephesus (Eph. 2:4-8) that "because of his great love for us, God, who is rich in mercy, made us alive with Christ even when we were dead in transgressions". And he "raised us up with Christ and seated us with him in the heavenly realms ... in order that in the coming ages he might show the incomparable riches of his grace, expressed in his kindness to us in Christ Jesus."

It should come as no surprise then to discover then that a Christian charity based in Wrexham has chosen to be known as Operation Kindness. Jesus invited people to follow him because his yoke is easy (*chrestos*) and it makes perfect sense that his followers would want to reach out into their communities in a similar way.

And yet the name does not have a biblical origin, as project leader Nick Pengelly explains. "Operation Kindness started as an umbrella organisation under which all the projects could run. It was set up separately from our church activities so that it could benefit the whole community and people could be involved in different projects and not have a Christian background. The name of the charity actually came from a children's book. In the middle of the story was the phrase 'and so Operation Kindness began' and this name seems to highlight the reason for the existence of the organisation."

The remit of the charity can be summarised as follows: "People are important." Operation Kindness aims to operate as a resource centre, developing a varied number of projects which are intended to develop the quality of life for people in the Wrexham area as the management team see gaps and possess the appropriate skills. In the same way the management team is keen to co-operate with other groups where they have the necessary expertise, with the desired aim of doing everything to the highest professional standards.

The charity has three trustees who take responsibility for ensuring that the charity complies with the requirements of the charity commission, but oversight of the projects has been delegated to a management team. From the very beginning the make up of this team has been seen as critical and the charity has sought to ensure that it includes people from a variety of professional backgrounds. A number of the team, for example, have experience of managing major projects, with one team member owning his own company. As a consequence time was given early on the development of a distinctive logo and a website (www.its-ok.org.uk), and one of the management team has specialised in funding and the researching of long-term grants.

The project attracted a number of small grants from local companies and organisations in its early stages, but according to Nick, "One of the initial struggles in starting any work is gaining experience and some history, which is needed to obtain significant funding. To get the work going has required significant funds but people are unwilling to give until some sort of track record can be demonstrated. This has been one of the most challenging aspects of the work and it would not have been possible without the ongoing support of the Community Church, which has supplied the bulk of the funding directly."

Dial a Friend, which offers a listening ear to lonely people is the core project of Operation Kindness. Research showed that there was only one other local helpline operating in North Wales. This NHS Help Line receives a large number of calls every month and volunteer Janet Roynon, who had been associated with it for several years, became the driving force of a ministry that does not pretend to have all the answers but hopes that listening and providing useful links can help callers make progress in the life issues they face.

As Nick explains, "We identified that the area lacking in helpline services was the simple friendship base linked to an opportunity for friendship groups. It is recognised that loneliness is a major stress issue. A simple phone call may make some difference, but ongoing friendship was vital. Many things may cause loneliness and isolation; bereavement is one example. Many professionals have seen the need for the service as it operates outside normal working hours when their services are limited."

The key areas covered by the helpline are listening, information, linking to a contact team or friendship groups, and small jobs in the local area. Once the target group had been identified and a genuine need exposed, a working group took on the task of ensuring that the helpline became a reality.

In a determined effort to ensure the highest possible standards, the management team decided that the project should in due course attain the full standards required by the National Help Line Association. For example, the volunteers were taken through basic training for phone line operators by the manager of the NHS CALL helpline and were taught to address any potential issues that they might have when handling a variety of challenging calls.

"You cannot provide effective friendship if you are prejudiced or judgemental," says Nick. "This was a challenging aspect for the call operations. Operators are also trained in how to handle difficult or abusive calls too."

In the same way, prior to the launch of the helpline, a committee set in place the necessary paperwork and established a secure environment as well obtaining confidentiality agreements. "And none of this would have happened in the time scale without the help of those who had experience of working in this kind of environment."

This is not to say there were no mistakes. "Our lack of experience meant that a number of things could have easily have been missed in the early stages," Nick says. "The need for a memorable number was missed and so we just took the next one on the list. It was 01978 35 35 35. In hindsight this turned out to be a great number, even though it is a little similar to the local taxi company."

The helpline was launched in January 2002 by Janet Ryder, the local Assembly member, and has also received enthusiastic support from the local MP. Advertising has been mainly through newspaper advertising and face-to-face contact.

An analysis of the calls over the first year showed that 60% came from newspaper adverts, 30% were referrals from other organisations and 10%

from posters in the library. Most callers lived in the Wrexham area and most calls were made early in the evening. Calls drop off over the two-hour period the service is manned (four nights per week). A small but very significant number of calls were made in the last ten minutes as people finally plucked up courage to call the line. An analysis of expressed needs has proved most reassuring as Nick explains. "It can be seen that we are successful in attracting calls, particularly from the people we are seeking to help. Some 49% expressed needs of loneliness; 10% simply wanted someone to listen and the same number were seeking practical help or wanted to be visited at home. Those suffering through bereavement (6%) were thought to be a significant group and we sought to help them by researching what was available in Wrexham. We found that there were long waiting lists (twelve months at CRUSE)."

In a determined effort to meet perceived needs Operation Kindness has also initiated a First Contact Team and its Breakthrough Friendship Groups. One of the key aims of the telephone line is to offer people a chance to break out of their loneliness and it often takes a number of calls before people will even begin to talk to someone. The First Contact Team seeks to assist in this process. The team is able to assess the specific needs of each caller and seeks to encourage them to join a Friendship Group if that is deemed appropriate. The project responded to the large number of older callers, for example, by establishing a group which caters for the over 60's.

Operation Kindness sees friendship as vital to any

society and consequently it aims to initiate different groups by linking people with similar outlooks together. The project currently runs three groups, each with their own committees, who take responsibility for organising games, talks and other social activities.

"The aim of each group is that they run themselves but have an association with Operation Kindness," Nick says. This association means that they keep certain standards and we are happy to direct people to them via the telephone line. Each person in the group is encouraged to look out for the others in the group because we believe they will find their own needs fulfilled as they give to others."

The groups have proved very successful too, with many people testifying that their lives have been changed through involvement in the groups. "Sandra for example (not her real name)," says Nick, "had nursed her husband through the final stages of cancer. Six months on she still could not face the outside world and she spent most of her time in tears, imprisoned in her home. Very nervously she came to a Breakthrough Friendship Group for the over 50's and was overwhelmed by the warmth of friendship. A few weeks later she told us, 'My daughter just can't believe the difference in me. I am so happy now'. Another person said that a number of people who had suffered bereavement were finding it difficult to break into a new group. This has now happened. The stories go on."

Janet, who is the founder and co-ordinator of the groups says, "When people get down they often tend to close the door on themselves and the solution is getting that door open and letting others into your lives, as much as anything else."

People can join the groups through personal contact or via the helpline. New groups will be set up across the area as need arises. There are currently three groups running in and around the Wrexham area but the project is also willing to work with partners in other places where the telephone line can be the link to help get them started in their locality. Future key goals are to maintain the profile of the service with focused advertising in all available media, to further build contact with professional service providers and other voluntary organisations, and to strengthen resources in the First Contact and practical areas of the service.

Muriel Spark once observed that she was a hoarder of two things - documents and trusted friends. She would certainly have felt at home in Wrexham. Operation Kindness offers us a very exciting and practical model because it shows that all we need is vision and commitment. Operation Kindness is certainly visionary. According to Nick Pengelly, charity status offers the possibility of obtaining larger grants, which can support the expansion of the telephone help line. As he says, "We see that there are many opportunities to move into a bigger area and are looking for partners to help this happen." The project is even willing to take risks and risk criticism by entering partnerships with those who are not of the faith. George Lings of the Sheffield Centre has suggested, "If we engage in the regeneration of communities because our gospel is for the whole person it will take significantly more money and human resources than we have. We shall have to move out of Christendom mode where we have called the shots and controlled the projects. In post-Christendom mode we have to dare to explore partnerships with others"[1].

Operation Kindness has experienced such a paradigm shift and is keen to be at the cutting edge of such a process according to Nick Pengelly. "The initial volunteers have been from within the church and we are looking to train more people who have no church connection. The project is for the community and not the church and we aim to see that this takes place. In the meantime every call makes another life slightly better."

E. Beyreuther wrote, "Kindness is an unmistakeable and essential characteristic of love. Because kindness is one of the chief gifts of the Spirit it becomes the subject of the exhortation of Colossians 3:12, 'Put on then as God's chosen ones, compassion and kindness'. As a direct outworking of *agape* it is always alive and active, breaking out spontaneously in the life of the man who is led by Christ. This completes the circle from the original kindness of God who created the world and men, separated a people for himself and remains kind despite sin and wickedness, to the revelation of his incomprehensible kindness of Jesus Christ in the fullness of time. Here God's saving activity reaches its goal. In Jesus Christ God's fatherly kindness can be seen as in a mirror. Moreover, the members of the Christian community, the church, have to choose as their path in the world the way of kindness which they must show to all men. At the same time they have to choose it in a world which often betrays little sign of it."[2]

It is to God's eternal glory that that divine characteristic is being reflected very clearly in Wrexham today.

PART 3
MAKING IT HAPPEN

by Iestyn Davies and Julian Richards

Chapter 7: Introduction

Part 1 of this book outlined why churches and Christian organisations should engage in social action. Part 2 has demonstrated that churches are already delivering programmes that impact communities and in doing so are providing everyday believers with an opportunity to demonstrate Christ's compassion. If we have succeeded so far it should have engaged you to such an extent that you will now be interested in practical guidance on how to commence a social project or expand your existing programme.

This section aims to give you a basic introduction to the principles shared by all successful community projects. In this respect the guidance that we pass on will not be limited to Christian projects but we will be seeking to see and express it through our experience of church and Christian organisations.

Like all good Christian preachers and teachers we will do this with the help of alliteration or at least the

3 "P's" of successful projects. They are:

- Planning and Profiling (Chapter 8)
- Pounds (Chapter 9)
- Partnership (Chapter 10)

Chapter 8 will examine some of the foundational questions one must address before starting any project. Specifically, it confronts us with the need to know our community and its needs so that we deliver projects that are actually needed rather than projects that we presume are needed.

Chapter 9 then moves on to look at developing a project from the perspective of the basic principles of fund raising.

Finally, chapter 10 will address the need for the church to develop strategic partnerships with others in order to be maximally effective. It examines the principle of partnership, its importance and concerns about being 'unequally yoked'.

In Part 4 we will examine a series of specific relationships, concentrating on the funding opportunities that these can provide.

In addressing these challenges we will try to break down some of the jargon associated with this field. Like all communities of interest, community development has built an amazing amount of terms and buzzwords. It is a field in which acronyms abound. There are also some peculiar idiosyncrasies about working within the church that impact upon how we engage in social programmes. We will try to explore how what we often term 'the world out there' can be reconciled to the world inside the walls of the church.

In each chapter we will also look at some of the potential pitfalls that relate to the way in which the secular and the sacred inter-relate. Unlike Part 1, these issues will be addressed from a practical as opposed to a theological perspective and in the context of the principles as they arise.

In this section we will cite examples from an imaginary fellowship: The Bethlehem Reformed, Presbyterian, Gospel Church of God (and Community Centre). And as they say in the movies, any resemblance to a church, living or dead, are totally intentional!

Chapter 8: Planning and Profiling

A call to entrepreneurship

There is a commonly used truism that goes something like this: "Those who fail to plan, plan to fail." And the truth is that the world is full of good ideas. Visionary people are ten a penny - they are commonly known as dreamers. What is in short supply, and the church is no different from the rest of society in this respect, is people who can take a good idea and actually deliver it in the everyday world.

This chapter will look at the principles of effective planning and the role played by community profiling programmes in particular. It is at the planning stage that the foundations are laid and as we are considering Christian projects it should come as no surprise that projects built on unsure foundations will not usually last even if they manage to get off the ground in the first place.

Community profiling or, Seeing through the eyes of the community

The key role of the social entrepreneur begins in reality not with a good idea but with the task of profiling the community. Churches haven't always been aware of the fact that they sometimes don't accurately reflect the diversity and general demography of their community. In a very real sense our community is often defined by the friendships and associations formed at church.

The church is in actual fact a community of interest. That is, it is a community that is defined and bound together not by geography but by an interest or experience in common. Other examples of communities of interest would include, say, the local bowls club or a support group for bereaved parents. By their very nature communities of interest and therefore the church can sometimes be a poor reflection of the wider world.

Effective churches by and large will be seeking to serve a geographical community, that is, a community extending beyond specific interests. However, it might seek to provide a specific programme to a key group of individuals or families. Often within funding bids and planning those who receive service are known as beneficiaries. It is important that any church at an early stage of its development of a community programme accepts the principle that the project exists for the beneficiaries, not for the church.

A healthy integrated church does however have a head start over many communities of interest. What binds a healthy church together is its concern with the needs of the wider community. Nevertheless take a look around at your neighbourhood; take a drive to the various districts of your town or city. If you live in a rural community ask yourself when was the last time that you met with someone not associated with your church or chapel. Community profiling begins with asking questions and with deferring observation until much later. Social scientists have perfected the art of defining communities statistically. It can be beneficial to sit and read the latest research and ask yourself from that perspective "how well do I know my community?"

Bethlehem Church in planning its new community programme could do worse than take a map of the town or area and, dividing it by local authority wards, assign a group or individual church member to write a one-page description of each based on the information available from government or local authority websites as well as personal reflection. The exercise could also form the basis of a prayer meditation. The only warning we would give to the good folk at Bethlehem is that they should undertake this exercise as if they lived (as some of the church membership no doubt does) in the wards in question. The church cannot be allowed to see the community it serves solely through its own eyes. It should appreciate it through the experiences of individual citizens living and working within it.

In more practical terms there is importance in

examining the local community at a ward level. Certain strategic funds are often directed to this lowest level of the community. It is also worth noting the names of individual councillors for each ward. Bethlehem might consider writing to each and asking them to list the three things a church could provide in their immediate locality. The things they list might not become a feature of any final community project, but what it will do is send a signal that Bethlehem is committed to serving its community and fostering relationships with its elected members.

Community profiling should enable the church to get a handle on its community. And at the end of the exercise the church should be able to identify key statistics, such as the number of school-age children, GCSE passes, unemployment rates, etc. It will have built up a useful database of statutory and voluntary agencies and, more importantly, a list of the key players, other social entrepreneurs, at work in the area.

Social entrepreneurs and the whole church

Much of the language of community development has by today come to include concepts and phrases more often associated with the world of business and commerce. This in many ways can seem disturbing and to some at least incongruous. However it does demonstrate the extent to which the developing of community projects has become professionalised and that its contribution to the economy of the country has been recognised.

In its favour, the concept of the social entrepreneur conveys something of the can-do spirit possessed by individuals who see themselves as personally committed to the process of developing projects that benefit society. Social entrepreneurs can be church leaders motivated by spiritual aims, businessmen who act out of a desire for profit but at the same time aim to improve their community, or the growing number of professional people employed to reinvigorate deprived areas and engage the socially excluded. What differentiates social entrepreneurs from business entrepreneurs is that profit is not the only or sole aim of their activity. What they share is a spirit of determination, commitment to excellence and the willingness to take risks.

Through history the church has furnished the world with great examples of social entrepreneurs. They still exist in fellowships today but the call to this form of spiritual ministry is often neglected within sermons and assessments of individuals' gifting. The church, communities and our nations need social entrepreneurs and in particular they need those driven by the grace of God. And at the heart of all successful projects there is at least one social entrepreneur, sometimes more.

Please take a moment to reflect on the content of this book so far. As you have thought over the theological basis for engagement and read about the successful projects described in Part 2, to what extent have you been challenged? The extent to which you can answer the challenge for social engagement will define your capacity to consider yourself a social entrepreneur.

Engaging the whole church

Whilst it is important to seek to develop social entrepreneurial gifting within parts of the church, it is important to recognise that a successful community project will only "get off the ground" if it is an integral part of the whole church. As already stated good ideas are not in short supply. Again what's needed are churches which are willing to make the fundamental readjustment needed to assure a strong foundation for the community projects.

Church, community and change

In walking through the process of Community Planning, and indeed the subsequent development of your project, Gweini partner Tearfund's 'Church, Community and Change' programme provides some very useful tools.

Tearfund
100 Church Rd
Teddington
TW11 8QE
020 8977 9144
www.tearfund.org.uk

Chapter 9: Funding Best Practice:

"He Who Pays the Piper"

During the numerous funding surgeries and individual consultations at Gweini we have come to realise that many churches see engaging in social programmes as a means of accessing government or independent trust funding. This is thoroughly understandable and even common sense. Governments and trusts expect that the voluntary sector to be drawn into providing services because of the funding available. But while it is possible in some instances to create a surplus, any church or voluntary group that engages in providing training, day-care or other activities will be best advised to see it as a sacrifice rather than an income generating exercise.

Before progressing any further it is best to clarify the two kinds of funding that projects can use, revenue funding and capital funding.

Types of funding

Revenue funding is income to pay running costs, purchase consumables such as stationery, and pay rent and bills. In some instances it can be used to pay for one-off costs such as computers and equipment, although it might be simpler to lease or rent equipment. It is not uncommon for larger funders to allow funds to cover the cost of mortgage interest payments. Often the most obvious revenue costs are salary and other employment related costs such as National Insurance and pension payments.

Capital funding on the other hand represents funding for larger items of equipment and improvements to facilities, such as the provision of a lift to allow access to an upper floor. Many areas of Europe have benefited from the European Regional Development Fund, which is one of the best examples of capital funding. The fund is aimed primarily to improve infrastructure and facilities. It is probably the most common source of European cash and many road bypasses have been funded by it. It is possible to receive capital support for the purchase of land or buildings and for expensive items. So for instance Bethlehem church could use capital funding to purchase a building as a community centre. If however it is also to be used as a church we can begin to see how things can become complicated. The funder would want to know which part of the capital funding is to be used for the aims of the community centre and what other resources are to be provided for the use of the same building as a church.

In this and indeed in all circumstances the key to following funding best practice is to respect the principle of **segregated funding**. Simply, this means that money received for a set purpose should only be used for the aims and objectives set out in the funding bid. Many voluntary sector projects sometimes find this difficult. But by opening separate bank account a degree of transparency can be brought to accounting procedures. It is also possible to set up new charities. For instance, Bethlehem could decide to set up the Bethlehem Charitable Trust specifically for the purpose of running its community project. At very least it should designate a separate account for its 'non-church' money and even consider appointing a special committee to manage this aspect of its ministry. There is nothing to stop Bethlehem Church billing Bethlehem Trust for the use of its facilities. Since the Trust is effectively paying rent to the church this cost is revenue rather than capital. Since revenue funding is easier to account for and sometimes easier to find, this arrangement might even be in both the Church's and the Trust's interests.

This of course raises some very interesting questions. Can the church sustain the division of its activity into community programme and worship and at the same time maintain a holistic mission? If control of the community programme is separated from the other aspects of the church's life, how can the fellowship as a whole own the vision? Incidentally there is no necessary reason why segregating accounts should lead to disenfranchising the congregation. It is important we believe that the fellowship as a whole is made aware of the need for financial accountability but this should not be allowed to lead to the conclusion that the community programme is somebody else's ministry.

More importantly, any church that decides to access funding, especially from government, will have to accept that the finance and the actual resources that it purchases don't really belong to the church. Rather the funding and resources belong to the beneficiaries for whom the money has been given. We wouldn't expect a church to raise finance for the Sunday School and spend it on a new set of crockery for the seniors' meeting. Likewise it would not be appropriate for a church to accept financial assistance for the provision of a CV writing club and use the facility solely for its men's club. But neither could funds for a daytime crèche for working parents be used to fund a homework club. Bethlehem, if it takes the financial assistance on offer, will have to accept the principle that as far as some aspects of its programme are concerned: "He who pays the piper calls the tune."

Equal opportunities

One of the most contentious issues in this area is the whole question of equal opportunities. For Gweini two principles are key to our understanding of these complicated questions.

The first principle is that "Jesus offered equal opportunities". Christ's earthly ministry involved engaging with all manner of socially undesirable people who often challenged the religious conventions of the period. This did not mean that he condoned sin but neither did he put a block on those who had obvious weaknesses from following him. The Christian gospel has always had to balance the need for righteousness with the generous application of grace. The truth is of course that while we might like to think that our churches are full of saints who never sin or fail to be tempted, this is naïve. We have to expect too that vulnerable people, so often the beneficiaries of social and community programmes, like us will carry personal and moral baggage. The difficulties that they find in overcoming these problems will often be in proportion to their challenging circumstances.

Let's put it another way. If Bethlehem is considering working in the field of HIV and Aids it will have to address the issue of serving people who are openly and unapologetically gay. If it is interested in offering help to substance misusers it will have to consider whether or not it wants to embrace harm minimisation, e.g. providing clean needles to heroin users or whether it wants to insist that all its clients are drug-free before providing services. Whilst consideration of the question of equal opportunities often surrounds the biggie questions such as sex, criminal behaviour and drug abuse it is worthwhile noting that at the heart of the principle is the question "who is the church providing the services for, the saint or the sinner?"

The second Gweini principle in respect of equal

opportunities is: "Social action is an authentic expression of worship." We do not see worship as distinct from providing practical assistance and compassion. Moreover it is from that heart of worship that acts of kindness flow. Worship is praise and adoration, what we do on a Sunday before the sermon, **and** it is the delivery of the parents and toddlers programme on a Monday morning. If the provision of services is as equally an act of worship and comparable to the preaching of a sermon, the leading of a Bible study or a time of worship, it is reasonable to require the same principles of biblical leadership from the person leading the lunch club as those in pastoral ministry or meeting leadership.

Before we consider the implications of this upon the way in which we approach equal opportunities criteria and funding, it might be beneficial to consider the way in which Bethlehem is to choose those who lead its community programme. In many fellowships the most cherished jobs are those that have the greatest limelight and in particular those that are expressed publicly on a Sunday or in meetings. Often it is a case of finding leaders for public ministry before finding those who are willing to lead the social programme.

For community action to become an integral part of its holistic church expression Bethlehem will need to ask itself which positions within the church leadership need to be filled first? Which areas of church life should members be encouraged to take up if the fellowship is to achieve its goals? Given that the church does not have a monopoly on social action it must also ask itself whether it is willing to release its members to work outside of the programme of the fellowship.

Despite our best efforts at Gweini our desire to press on beyond the considerations of equal opportunities is not always met. This is due in no small part to the fact that the equal opportunities criteria are often invoked to deny funding to church and overtly Christian projects. This we believe is due in part to the way in which Christian groups address the issue as well as a misunderstanding on the part of funders. It is however a reflection on the extent to which a secular world view has overtaken our culture.

As this book is being written, the UK government has just finished consulting on the implementation of the European Union's Equal Opportunities Directive. The applicability of EU Directives is limited unless the domestic government passes legislation to incorporate it into UK law. To give effect to the directive the UK government is about to pass a law that will allow groups in limited circumstances to appoint only members of their faith or belief to employment positions. It will not allow discrimination on the grounds of beneficiaries, that is, those receiving assistance.

In our opinion it will also be worthwhile churches differentiating between the kinds of employment on offer. In some instances the creation of employment is an acceptable aim of the programme. Whilst it would be acceptable therefore to appoint a Christian to a position, say, of manager of a scheme recycling old furniture, it would not be appropriate to state as the project's aims the creation of ten jobs or even volunteering positions and restrict employment just to members of the religion.

Let us look at this scenario in more detail drawing on the definitions and principles of "P is for Planning". Let us suppose that Bethlehem is really embarking upon a project, which aims to create employment opportunities via recycling old furniture. The aim of the project is to create skilled craftspeople who understand not only upholstering techniques but also environmental sustainability.

In its funding bid and project basis it sets the strategic aim of creating ten jobs. If it forgets to state in its project basis that three positions are management then it would have difficulty in applying the criteria of belonging to the Christian faith as a condition of employment. We can expect the appointment of Christian managers to be interpreted as a proportionate measure to maintain the ethos of the scheme. The effect Bethlehem's plans have upon the project however, is to reduce the number of direct beneficiaries from ten to seven, i.e. the number of positions open to all applicants. Since it has now limited the number of beneficiaries it has failed to comply with principles of equal opportunities and failed to meet its key objective of creating ten jobs open to all. This in itself will have implications for its outcomes and also for the cost per beneficiary for the project, so it will probably be over budget. The three staff employed within the ethos of the project are indirect beneficiaries.

If however, it wants to maintain the prospect of creating ten jobs open to all applicants, i.e. to have ten direct beneficiaries, it must ensure that it plans from the outset for the management element that enables it to employ members of the Christian faith. In other words, it has to make 13 jobs. Seeking to find a practical way around these difficulties and again to provide clarity, it could be conceivable that the Bethlehem Trust agrees an equal opportunities policy that encapsulates this principle - whereas the church itself might not wish to do so. It would also have to ensure that at the planning stage it allows for sufficient funding to employ all staff and cover the employment and training costs for its beneficiaries.

Public, private and match funding

Perhaps put off by the prospect of too much form filling and equal opportunities, Bethlehem considers following a separate route, which would involve understanding of the various kinds of funding sources. The eldership, drawing on the principles of European Funding, are learning to differentiate between public funding, private funding and match funding. Each form of funding has an important part to play in securing the short, medium and long-term sustainability of a community project.

Private funding is the form of funding most familiar to churches. This is the income that comes from tithes, offerings and sacrificial giving. It can also come in the form of legacies and bequests. This is by and large an unrestricted fund as the giver is making the donation to the church in general. (Restricted funds are those that can only be used for a specific purpose.)

An often under-used feature of private funding is Gift Aid. This is a facility that allows registered charities to gain an additional 28% on gifts from private givers who are taxpayers. In the case of higher rate taxpayers there are also personal advantages to giving tax efficiently through Gift Aid. It must be remembered however, that gifts via schemes such as the Charities' Aid Foundation Charity Card and Sovereign Giving have already received an additional income from the Chancellor of the Exchequer and that the charity receiving the gift cannot claim the further amount.

Gifts made from legacies or bequests cannot be treated for Gift Aid and often come with strings attached. Increasingly families are requesting gifts to be given to charity in lieu of floral tributes at funerals. Whilst it might not always be appropriate during a time of mourning to raise the specifics of how a gift should be used, consideration should be given to being able to account for these gifts in an open manner. It is worthwhile discussing within the fellowship the issue of how to give effectively upon death.

Gone are the days of sales of work, and charity shops have replaced jumble sales. The whole issue of **fundraising** is worthwhile examining in depth as special legal restrictions apply to how it is carried out. The best source guidance on the issue can be gained from the Charity Commission website. It is highly unlikely that most churches would have a genuine need to employ the facilities of a fundraising consultant and all charities should be wary of those who promise millions of pounds of new money overnight. Due to the fact that the principles of balance sheets and nominal ledgers leave most of us in the dark we would recommend any project commencing or expanding its work to identify qualified and experienced treasurers or even to appoint auditors. It is worthwhile bearing in mind that charities with incomes in excess of £100,000 must have appointed auditors. Most funders would expect to see these appointments in place before an application that takes the organisation over the mandatory threshold is accepted. Many fellowships hold thank offerings or gift days and whilst we would thoroughly agree that all our resources belong to the Lord we would underline the need to ensure that when gifts are solicited for an express purpose that they are used for that purpose. Honesty and integrity applies as equally to gifts given within the fellowship as to those sought from without.

Other sources of private funding come from corporations, grant awarding trusts and members of the public. Directories of funders are available and are often held by local CVCs. The membership fee for joining could prove a worthwhile investment. Many trusts will however not support unsolicited appeals. Others operate elaborate bidding procedures, while some can be applied for simply by letter and a brief project outline accompanied by a budget breakdown. The only way to know how to approach individual trusts is to contact them requesting further information.

The benefits of approaching independent and private trusts is that the procedures for accessing grants can be a lot simpler than that for statutory based money. Gifts can also be sought from local businesses, and many larger corporations operate charitable schemes within their location. Again, an approach is best made directly to the company, probably to the Managing Director in the case of smaller companies, and to the public relations department when seeking assistance from larger concerns.

Often after having embarked on successful smaller projects a church or Christian project might seek to gain financial assistance from a government department or from Europe. In the first Gweini publication Dan Boucher listed the numerous grants and funding schemes available within Wales.[3]

Bethlehem church is based in what is known as a Communities First area (see Part 4). As its first attempt at attracting **public funding** it chooses to start with this funding stream. The church has decided to launch a community internet café and hopes that the experience of meeting together and learning to access the Internet will develop self-esteem, confidence and enable beneficiaries of the project to gain specific computer skills. However the fellowship realises that it is not sufficient to simply plug in a few computers in a café area of the church. A key element of the Communities First funded project is that the project has to deliver results that meet priorities of the

Communities First Action Plan, which addresses the Communities First key themes. We can see how the process of applying for and administering public funding is far more complicated than private trust funding or utilising money already within the church. However, with the help of a Communities First officer and through support from other organisations, Bethlehem does find the process worthwhile and succeeds in gaining assistance.

A feature of the Communities First programme is that the support from the Welsh Assembly Government requires what is known as **match funding**. This means that only a proportion of the total budget for the internet café will come from the government. In other words, Bethlehem will only receive say £5,000 out of a total project budget of £7,000. In these circumstances the church could choose to apply to a private trust for the remaining £2,000, or it could use its own resources or (if the eldership is in agreement!) apply to a lottery-based trust for further support. (Incidentally, money from the many lottery-funded trusts is described as public funding, which perhaps gives weight to the belief held by many people that the lottery is actually a form of taxation and one which is primarily aimed at the poor.)

The value of capital

The Gweini network of churches represents tremendous **social capital**. This social capital is an investment made by the largely unpaid volunteer time of men and women across Wales. What is true for Gweini and Wales is equally true of all churches across the UK and beyond.

What do we mean by social capital? The church 'invests' its time and energy into its communities. Unlike 'hard' capital, i.e. money or resources, social capital can best be expressed as the multiplied value of vital relationship between an individual or a group and their physical and social environment. It is an individual's capacity to engage and contribute, not purely in financial terms but in and of themselves.

Just as businesses need and value capital in order to invest and get off the ground, so communities need social capital invested in them in order to see regeneration, renewal and answers to the pressing social problems that we live with each day. In healthy and socially prosperous communities social transactions take place: the free flowing of ideas, support and encouragement, as well as business transactions designed to bring about a profit.

Many people would have grave doubts about thinking of individuals as possessing, or indeed being, 'capital'. At some point we could discuss the implications of this notion further. But for now we will have to concern ourselves with the implications of the concept for successful projects. Without an investment of social capital alongside hard cash, projects fail and communities experience an increased sense of loss and disengagement.

Whilst the church is aware of its capital resources

such as cash, buildings and other assets, much of its social capital often languishes uninvested and disengaged. Or in many cases its social capital is invested solely in the church and not beyond. We could argue that there is a parallel between the notion of social capital and the concept of the talents as outlined in the gospels. Unless the talent in each of us, or in these terms our social capital, is invested wisely we will not see rewards.

The concept of social capital can be demonstrated to some extent by an examination of the way in which European Structural Funds treat the contribution made by both staff and volunteers to a particular project.

European funds need to be matched by resources originating in the country of benefit. Despite the fact that in some areas Europe via the domestic government will fund up 70% of a project's total cost, many voluntary sector and indeed commercial sector projects would find it hard to provide the necessary match funding. Therefore it was important to identify a way of supporting the investment emanating from Europe. This is called funding in-kind and while the concept was not entirely new, for many social entrepreneurs this is where we first came across the principle.

Fred, a volunteer on an ICT project for kids, is also a network administrator for a large corporation. When Fred contributes his time and expertise to the kids' computer project at his local church, the project can 'cash in' the notional value of his time at professional rates and use it as match funding. (If you have been following the thread of the plot so far you will see how this is in fact private match funding as it comes from a private source, i.e. Fred's own time.) It is important to note however, if Fred contributed his time only, say, as a play-worker then it is at this rate that his contribution could be calculated.

However, this is not the complete picture. A basic calculation of the benefit of Fred's time cannot account for its value as social capital. It cannot calculate the benefit Fred provides the young people as he shares his experience of growing up in the same town and facing the same challenges. Fred is investing something of himself in his community. This aspect of social capital introduces us to the notion of **added value**. In recent years funders, whether they are statutory, European or indeed private funders have come to recognise the value of social capital as beyond its cash value - it has added value. The attraction of defining investment in terms of social capital is that it allows the project and funders to assess, however subjectively, more than the pounds and the pence.

Moreover, investing social capital increases social capital. It is not just the volunteers and staff of community projects that have a value. Naturally beneficiaries also have social capital. When we enable a single mum to learn new skills or help someone with low self esteem raise their self-awareness, we bring about an increase in their social capital. It is as if a sum of money has been taken from the box under the floorboards and placed in the hands of a skilful stockbroker. Perhaps, to put it in more biblical terms, the innate God-given value of each individual has been brought to the fore.

The church should not be surprised by the principle, which says the more we give of ourselves the more our communities benefit. It is at the heart of the concept of incarnational ministry. As already mentioned, social transactions are at the heart of community and it should come as no surprise therefore that reserves of social capital are one of our churches' greatest resources.

In practical terms, when Bethlehem comes to explain the value of a project to a funder or when its leaders are in a strategic partnership, talking in terms of developing, investing and utilising social capital is key. It is a way of showing that they understand the latent self worth of individuals. Key words and phrases for them and us to bear in mind are "developing social capital" and "adding value to financial resources through utilising social capital".

Chapter 10: The Power of Partnership

Partnership is a key area of community development work. There is a temptation for churches to think that nobody else is doing anything in the community or doing anything of real worth. Sometimes as Christians we can believe that it's only a church project that can make a difference. This can very easily cause us to set up our projects in isolation.

Working independently is a big 'no-no' in community development terms, in fact it breaks nearly all community development rules in one go. If you want to create hostility in your community, step on people's toes and gain a bad reputation as a community organisation, there's one easy way to do it. Work independently, set up a project without consultation, launch it without anybody out there knowing about it, and you'll achieve all these things.

Many churches are hesitant about the concept of working in partnership with the secular world, because there is a fear of being "unevenly yoked" or being controlled by others and therefore compromising the faith. At this point it may be helpful to point out that partnership is not merger, it's not losing one's distinctives. Partnership is strategising together, talking together, sharing resources where possible, and not duplicating one another's projects. It's avoiding competition for funds and it's ensuring best value for money on behalf of the clients and beneficiaries.

Partnership is essential if you want to draw any government funding down on your project. These days, evidence that you're communicating, consulting and not duplicating is essential criteria for many grant-giving bodies. In our experience at Cornerstone church, we have found that partnership is not only key for funding, but it's an open door for creating influence in the community. When one works independently, the only people we can influence are ourselves or our beneficiaries. When one works in partnership, we share our salt and light, our wisdom, our good practice and our lives with other agencies working in the field.

It has been a principle of Cornerstone Church to work in partnership from the very beginning. Our first partnership was with a local Anglican church. We wanted to do a holiday kids club, but we were a very young church and had no church hall or premises to work in. The Anglican church was a somewhat older church and had no team but had a church hall. We approached them and said, "We'll run the club for you, and you provide the hall." They jumped at the chance!

This single decision benefited us in the following ways:

1. It removed suspicion amongst local churches and the local community concerning Cornerstone being a new church and being unknown.
2. It gave Cornerstone credibility and a safety factor as we worked alongside a trusted, known and established organisation, in this case the Anglican church.
3. We benefited from profile and publicity in the wider area that we were working in.

After buying our premises, we decided to hold adult education classes in the evening. The first thing we did was contact the local college and university that were already running such classes in the local community at various premises. We could have run adult education classes by ourselves, but we decided to do it in partnership with the college and the university, and the following benefits resulted:

1. We provided a room to the college and they paid for it.
2. The college provided us with laptops and computers, and a qualified teacher to run the computer course.
3. The college supplied the advertising, administration and the registration process for the course.
4. We became known as a church that hosted adult education classes. People came to our centre and our reputation grew as a provider in the community - easy!

One of the most strategic things we did was connect with a local development group, consisting of agencies, community residents, local authority representatives, police and education personnel. Such groups meet together to develop coherent strategy in your area. Some of these groups are embryonic, some are linked to large, non-profit making organisations or a development trust. These groups have influence, are powerful and are very strategic.

We decided to go along to the embryonic launch of our local community development group. The meetings were dull and often contentious and very long, but we decided to stick in there. Over the years Cornerstone has become a key player in this development group, that now has formed into a large development trust consisting of maybe 30 or 40 agencies, local authority, police and education and community representatives. I was invited to chair this group and it has proved to be a strategic area of influence for us as a church. What does it mean for us as a local church?

1. We are a key player in the community.
2. We are accepted and respected.
3. We have credibility to fund our projects.
4. We have leadership influence in our community.

Partnership is not only essential for funding and delivering projects that are in the interest of the community we wish to serve, but also strategic in networking, building relationships and influencing policy for our community.

The way ahead

Here are some points that may help you discover partnerships in your area:

1. Telephone your local authority and ask to speak to someone responsible for community development in your area.
2. Ask to meet with your local councillor and explain your desire to serve your community and get involved.
3. Contact your local County Voluntary Council (CVC) (see Part 4) and ask who to contact in your area concerning community development. Are there any community development groups taking place in your area?

PART 4
PARTNERING WITH WHO, AND HOW?

By Daniel Boucher

Having considered the importance of partnership we now move to consider the key bodies with whom we must partner.

- Local Government
- County Voluntary Councils (CVCs)
- The National Assembly for Wales
- Welsh European Funding Office (WEFO)

We cannot understand how to engage with these bodies until we understand something about them, how they operate and what they have to offer. In what follows, therefore, we will consider the above bodies, giving the lion's share of our attention to local government, given its prime importance for the local voluntary sector.

Chapter 11: Partner One: Local Government

In the mid twentieth century the norm/aspiration was that local government was a service provider. As the amount of money spent by local authorities became greater, however, central government began to impose new spending restraints through a number of rather technical sounding procedures: Compulsory Competitive Tendering (CCT), followed by Best Value, and now something called the Wales Programme for Improvement. These have increasingly compelled local authorities to stop providing local services themselves and instead to buy services from companies and the voluntary sector. Local government has become increasingly dependent on the voluntary sector, especially in the provision of social services.

In the new environment there was a nearly threefold increase in local authority money going to voluntary sector projects in Wales between 1990-1999. The total amount of local authority funding to the voluntary sector for the year 1998/9 was £29 million, which works out at an average of £10 per head of population.[4] This clearly demonstrates a new funding trend/opportunity that the Christian voluntary sector has been so slow to recognise and benefit from.

Funding streams

It is not possible for a resource such as this to provide a comprehensive overview of all the funding streams provided by local authorities, with which the Christian voluntary sector could engage. Money is organised differently in different local authorities and thus the reader will need to research his or her own local authority funding streams to establish the potential bidding opportunities. Having said this, however, some important general points can be made. Most local authority funding falls into one of two categories: small community grants, accessed by relatively small community projects, and the larger grants or contracts. This category of funding provision constitutes the largest local government investment in the voluntary sector, although the voluntary sector shares monies flowing from these opportunities with private companies that also seek contracts.

Small grants

For the purpose of providing a taster of small local authority funding streams, the community grants provided by Carmarthen County Council are listed below:

- Community Chest Capital Scheme
- CCC Cultural Grants
- CCC Leisure Grants
- Education Grants
- Social Grants

- Pensioners Grant
- Pride in our Youth
- Welsh Church Fund
- Sportlot Community Chest

The Welsh Church Act funds

There is not the space to look at each funding stream in turn but, given its significance to the church and presence across the whole of Wales, the Welsh Church Act funds deserves further examination. Section 19 of the Welsh Church Act 1914, which led to the disestablishment of the Church in Wales, made provision for the funding of church and other cultural projects.

Today the money made available from this stream is actually very limited. Its Grants tend to be small, amounting to between a few hundred and a few thousand pounds, although they can be as large as £3,000. Having said this, however, in aggregate the money still amounted to a very significant £500,000 for 1998-99. In an age where being a Christian voluntary sector project can make accessing funding difficult, it is encouraging that there is still a fund, resting on an Act of Parliament, that is defined in terms of the church. This is not to suggest that the money all goes to churches. In 1998-89 it was estimated that £250,000 went to non-church projects. The fact, however, that there is a fund defined in terms of the church, that invests 50% of its monies in the church is not to be dismissed.[5]

WELSH CHURCH ACT FUNDS
Where to apply

If you live in:
- Blaenau Gwent
- Caerphilly
- Newport
- Torfaen

Your Welsh Church Fund money is administered by Monmouthshire Council

If you live in:
- Bridgend
- Merthyr Tydfil

Your Welsh Church Fund money is administered by Rhondda Cynon Taff

If you live in:
- Cardiff

Your Welsh Church Fund money is administered by the Vale of Glamorgan

Major funding streams, partnerships and plans

Key areas of local authority service provision are presided over by a number of partnerships, each of which has a plan outlining the priorities and projected policy actions in that area, whose implementation it monitors. Partnerships are particularly significant because, unlike local authority committees, which only include councillors, partnerships often offer seats around the table to the voluntary sector. Increasingly they are formed on the basis of the **three-thirds principle**, which prescribes that policy should be applied through 'partnerships' consisting of one-third politicians, one-third local government officers/officials and one-third the private/voluntary sector. As one examines local government activities one becomes aware that the potential interface for the Christian voluntary sector is very extensive.

Local authority plans/partnerships exist on three levels, which we will consider in ascending order from the bottom up.

1) Operational delivery plans

These include:

- Health Services Plans
- Local Action Teams (drug and alcohol)
- Social Care Plans
- Children's Services Plans

- Children First
- Early Years and Childcare Partnership Plans
- Young People's Partnership Plans
- Behaviour Support Plan
- Youth Justice Plans
- Careers Service
- Housing Operational Plan[6]

2) Thematic strategic plans

These include:

- Drug and Alcohol Teams
- Crime Reduction Strategy
- Education Strategic Plans
- Young People's Partnership Strategy
- Local Housing Strategy
- Local Transport Plans

Examination of these plans is of great importance because it reveals the actual interface between local government and the voluntary sector. Many of these plans are developed, implemented and monitored by partnerships and many of these partnerships operate on the basis of the three-thirds principle or something like it and will thus involve the voluntary sector.[7] If you have a special area of interest then contact your local authority to find out about the relevant plan and to establish whether it has a partnership and whether this involves the voluntary sector.

In considering these lower tiers of plans one must be aware that there is a general desire to streamline and reduce the number of plans/partnerships. Furthermore, one should also be aware that the list of plans is an approximation by the National Assembly of local government plans. On the ground in your particular local authority they may go by different names and in some cases be organised differently.

3) Local level universal frameworks[8]

Subsidiary universal frameworks include

a) Children and Young People's Frameworks

The Children and Young People's Framework outlines the priorities of the local authority. This gives rise to a Children and Young People's Partnership wherein seats will be allocated according to the three-thirds principle between local government/the wider statutory sector, business and the voluntary sector. The partnership has the task of bidding for and then allocating the very substantial funds from Cymorth - the Children and Young People's Support Fund.

The **Children and Young People's Support Fund** is an extremely important funding stream for the Christian voluntary sector. It began life in the financial year 2003-2004 and currently has an indicative allocation for the first year of £35 million. In the words of the Social Inclusion Report: "This funding programme has been developed on the basis of research evidence which shows that targeted support for children and young people can improve the life chances of children from disadvantaged families."[9] Cymorth "will fund project work and some central infrastructure costs within the following themes for activity":

- Family support
- Health promotion
- Play, leisure and enrichment
- Empowerment, participation and active citizenship
- Community development
- Training, mentoring and information
- Building childcare provision
- Inclusion and access

b) Strategic Plans/Partnerships for Health and Well Being

Organised again on the basis of the three-thirds principle, these partnerships provide yet another interface through which the Christian voluntary sector can engage.

The NHS Plan set out an initial commitment to create Strategic Partnerships for health and wellbeing. The Implementation Group has taken this concept forwards, and proposes **that there should be a new statutory duty on each local authority and Local Health Board, to come together to develop and implement a Strategy for Health and Well-being in their area.** "They will be required to co-operate with each other, and to work in consultation with a wide range of local interests. These should include the relevant NHS trusts, and service providers in the independent and voluntary sectors; patient, user and carer groups; the voluntary sector; and a wide range of related service interests including housing, education and community development. Specialist public health involvement will be essential to this process."[10]

Given the role played by the Christian voluntary sector in the promotion of health and wellbeing, and the contribution that the sector has to make to the development of an enlightened understanding of well-being, the Health and Well-being Strategy and Partnership constitute an important potential area for our engagement.

Community strategies

The local level universal framework comprises of one strategy that overarches all local government competencies, the Community Strategy and one partnership, the Local Strategic Partnership (LSP).

Community Strategies constitute one of the most significant determinants of what local authorities will actually do. As the guidance to local authorities for developing the Community Strategy makes plain, the Community Strategy 'should be central to an authority's planning and resource decision, ensuring that local priorities and concerns are reflected in the allocation of resources. Members who are responsible for developing policies and strategies, proposing the allocation of resources and taking decisions on behalf of the Council will need to translate priorities arising from the community strategy into a clear set of activities for the Council, and ensure that resources are allocated to deliver the specific actions to which the authority has committed itself.'[11]

There are two bases for engagement with the Communities Strategies process:

1) Community planning meetings

In an attempt to engage with as great a part of the community as possible in the development of the strategy, local authorities arrange a whole series of community planning meetings within which any community group/member of the public can engage.

2) Local strategic partnerships

Far more significantly, however, at the heart of the Community Strategies process are the 'Local Strategic Partnerships' (LSPs), which, formed on the basis of the three-thirds principle, involves voluntary and community groups. It is the purpose of the LSP to both shape the Community Strategy, in consultation with the wider community, and to monitor its implementation. As a key salt and light position, membership of the LSP must be a major priority for the church/Christian voluntary sector.

Regardless of whether one can obtain membership of the LSP, however, engagement with the Community Strategy process is important for the following reasons:

Influencing local government priorities

Given that the Community Strategy is the overarching plan in relation to which all others are made accountable and in relationship to which all funding streams ultimately relate, engagement with the Community Strategy is vital for a church that wants to be salt and light to the local community. It provides a clear opportunity to inform the definition of your local authority's priorities and thus spending.

Faith Communities

Government guidance specifically encourages local authorities to engage with faith communities in the development of community strategies. '**Specific efforts should be made to involve** different ethnic communities, women, **faith communities**, older people and disabled people who have a positive contribution to make to the future development and well being of their communities.'[12] Interestingly the Local Government Association (not to be confused with the Welsh Local Government Association) is also clear that faith communities are an important dimension of society with which local authorities must engage in the development of Community Strategies. Having reflected on the Community Strategies process they observe: 'All this provides considerable opportunities for the faith communities to get involved. They will have a specific contribution to make to the development of a long-term vision for the area and will want to ensure they make an active contribution during the consultation process on the development of the Community Strategy.'[13]

While government guidance does not say explicitly that local authorities should have faith communities representation in Local Strategic Partnerships, the fact that it has made a clear statement about the importance of engaging with faith communities strengthens our position in arguing that the LSP should have faith communities representation. How can an LSP be a vehicle for community leadership if it leaves out a key sector of the community? As a body with representation in every community across Wales, the church must be included.

Developing key relationships

Perhaps more significantly for practical purposes, the implications of the church demonstrating its concern about the future development of its community, and readiness to come out of its building and develop relationships with wider civil society, is hugely important. Quite apart from anything else, the development of such relationships means that when you are looking for funding you are not an unknown body. Indeed, if you have a relationship and have demonstrated a real interest and capacity to make a difference, you may even find that the Council, or partnerships that it facilitates, approach you proactively.

The development of Community Strategies presents the church/Christian Voluntary sector in Wales (and indeed the UK as a whole) with a new foundation upon which to engage with society, to develop key relationships and become a community pivot. Furthermore, it presents a challenge that only the **local** Christian voluntary sector and local church can effectively respond to. Whilst it will not be possible for Gweini to engage directly in each local authority, it does hope that this, and other Gweini resources, will help equip the local Christian voluntary sector to make an effective response. This 'influencing/relationship developing strategy' of engagement is never easy, especially in the context of rising political correctness, but that is precisely why we need to engage.

Further opportunities for engagement

Having considered the interface provided by the three tiers of local government plans and partnerships, it is important to recognise that not all potential interfaces for the Christian voluntary sector with local authorities can be collapsed into this window on local government. Some crucial interfaces can only be seen by looking beyond these plans.

The Local Government Voluntary Sector Compact

One new challenge for the Christian Voluntary sector is the development of the Voluntary Sector Compact process.

In 1998 the Government negotiated national compacts between itself and the voluntary sector. Compacts were agreed between Government and the Welsh, Scottish, Northern Irish and English voluntary sectors. The Welsh Compact provides the foundation for a potentially intimate relationship between the Assembly and the voluntary sector. It moves away from the old representative model of democracy by explicitly conferring rights of representation to voluntary organisations.[14] Thus even though no one elected them in the conventional sense, there is an important sense in which voluntary sector representatives have become politicians in a way that was not possible in the old order.

The Compact also enumerated other commitments. Government undertook to make the voluntary sector aware of funding opportunities, to meet regularly with the sector and listen to its ideas for policy development, whilst the voluntary sector undertook to share its best practice and to operate highly professional management practices.[15]

In 1999 the then Secretary of State for Wales, Alun Michael announced that all Welsh local authorities and quangos must also negotiate compacts with the voluntary sector, thus further extending the profile and influence of the sector. On this point interestingly Wales led the way. It was not until 2000 that the UK government announced a similar policy for all British local authorities. Today all local authorities have compacts in place, but sadly the Christian voluntary sector has had little (if any in most places) input into the negotiation process.

More significant than the definition of the compact, however, is the creation of the 'Compact Monitoring Group'.[16] *They include politicians, voluntary sector representatives and local government officers and it is their purpose to monitor the implementation of the compact. These bodies can be very significant and where Christians have obtained membership this has been of strategic importance especially in deconstructing fears about the Christian voluntary sector.*

The membership of your Compact Monitoring Group has almost certainly already been determined but membership is for fixed periods and so vacancies will arise. It is important to seek membership because:

1. It helps to make local government and the wider voluntary sector aware that the church/Christian voluntary sector is still a very significant part of society.

2. It gives us an opportunity to inform local government policy/priority with the perspective of the Christian voluntary sector.

3. It means that we will be more aware of secular funding opportunities both those emanating from government and elsewhere.

4. It gives us an opportunity to build relationship with government and the wider voluntary sector so that we can demythologise concerns about faith based projects.

The imperative for our engagement in the Compact Monitoring Group underlines the imperative for our engagement with the County Voluntary Council (see next section) since it is this body that determines membership of the Monitoring Group.

LA21 Strategy

An LA21 strategy is a document and process that seeks to demonstrate how a local authority will champion **sustainable development**, namely an economic growth that neither harms the natural nor the social environment, since such damage will undermine growth in the long term. Most Church projects uphold and champion relationships and thus the local social environment. To this extent they can be said to promote sustainable development and the interests of the LA 21 initiative. Some church projects will of course also have a direct positive impact upon the natural environment.

Shaping your LA21 strategy

Ask your local authority for a copy of the LA21 strategy. Does it give equal weighting to the natural and the social environment? Does it provide a sensible definition of the social environment?[17] Do any of your church projects have some best practice that could add to the document? Arrange a meeting with your LA 21 officer and responsible councillor to demonstrate your interest. Explain how your church plays a key role promoting the social environment in your area. What would the effect be on your community if the church was not there? Talk about how sustainability can be taken forward in your area. Ask if there is anything that you can do to promote understanding about the role of LA21 in your locality.

Promoting LA21

In addressing sustainable development in the context of local authorities one should be aware that LA 21 is struggling to get off the ground in some areas. Many people have still never heard of it or do not know what it means. The local government officers charged with the responsibility of making sustainability a reality are always looking for enthusiastic community stakeholders willing to take a lead in community regeneration and LA21 in their area.

There is a real opportunity for church projects here to both raise their profile in a way that places the church very much on the cutting edge of community regeneration, and to build constructive relationship/ partnerships with councillors and local government officers looking for helpful community stakeholders to make LA 21 a reality in their area.

One way you could put the church at the cutting edge of your community would be by suggesting the creation of a LA21 roundtable/forum of local community stakeholders. Such bodies have been created at different tiers of government to monitor sustainability and advise government on policy development in this area. As the source of such an idea you would be well placed to have a significant role within such a body.

Faith communities: a guide to best practice

In drawing this section to a close it would be remiss not to make reference to an important development in England that could be appropriated by Wales. Perhaps the most significant document to ever be written by government on the relationship between religious bodies and local government was published in February 2002, *Faith and Community: A Guide to Best Practice*. It makes a whole series of very important commitments which could significantly impact the relationship between the church/Christian voluntary sector and local government.

Faith and Community is significant for:

1. Underlining the importance of involving faith communities in the development of community strategies
2. Stressing the importance of local authorities involving faith communities in local government Voluntary Sector Compacts.
3. Generally raising the profile of religious bodies in the context of local government.
4. Raising the profile of faith-based welfare.
5. Making it clear that it can be appropriate to fund faith-based projects.
6. Proposing the institutionalisation of dialogue between local government and religious bodies.
7. Suggesting new appointments in local government to develop its relationship with faith communities.

From a Welsh perspective the difficulty with this document is that it was produced by the

Local Government Association (whose jurisdiction is England), not the Welsh Local Government Association. At the time of writing it does not apply in Wales and so it would not have been appropriate for this chapter to examine it in detail. Having said this, given its significance and the hope that it might be applied either wholly or partially in Wales, it seems appropriate to draw attention to it.

FAITH AND COMMUNITIES

To get a copy of *Faith and Community* visit the Local Government Association website and click on their publications icon.

www.lga.gov.uk

To read Christian analysis of *Faith and Community* see the final section of -
The Church and Local Government in the 21st Century: Mastering the Shift from Government to Governance, PQ, March 2002, Evangelical Alliance, Public Affairs, Whitefield House, 186 Kennington Park Rd, London.

Chapter 12: Partner Two: The Wider Voluntary Sector

It is now important to turn to consider the churches' relationship with the wider voluntary sector. This is of critical importance for a number of reasons:

In the first instance we will benefit from the friendship and **best practice** of the wider voluntary sector.

More importantly, however, for the purposes of accessing **funding**, some funding streams are allocated with a view to strengthening local civil society and thus require funding applications to be made by 'partnerships' of different projects. This is not to say that a particular project cannot maintain its distinctive identity, but that it must bid for the money in partnership with other distinctive projects. This requires relationship.

Furthermore, to the extent that politicians and civil servants increasingly look for guidance from civil society groupings such as the voluntary sector, it is vital that we are located under the recognised voluntary sector umbrella, that our **voice** may be heard.

Leaving our 'parallel universe'

Persuading the church to engage with the wider voluntary sector is more difficult than encouraging it to engage with traditional political institutions for two reasons.

In the first instance, to the extent that engaging with government is something that we all have to do to by virtue of being electors and tax payers, there is less distance for some of us to travel in developing relationship with government bodies. Whilst Jesus taught that we should pay taxes (Matt. 22:21) and Paul that government was instituted by God (Rom. 13:1-7), nothing of this kind was ever said about the secular voluntary sector.

In the second instance, while the secular voluntary sector is a body whose remit overlaps with our own, many projects often seem to have what might be described as a post-Christian, politically correct value system.

In responding to these concerns, however, we must remember that we are not just called to be salt and light to government but to the world as it is. This will not be achieved if we build a 'parallel universe', Christian voluntary sector ghetto. To this extent it is vital to understand that Gweini was not established for the purpose of servicing such a ghetto. It was formed for the purpose of representing the Christian voluntary sector to, and building relationships with, the government and the wider voluntary sector, in order that the Christian voluntary sector can take its 'salt and light' seat in the wider voluntary sector/civil society.

County Voluntary Councils

In light of the need to engage with the broader voluntary sector in order to be salt and light to the world and to enjoy funding opportunities, Gweini would urge all church or para-church projects to join their local County Voluntary Council (CVC).

We need to put the Christian voluntary sector on local government's radar screen. County Voluntary Councils are funded by their local authority to support the sector and represent its interests in the local political process. If church projects do not join, then local government presumes that the church is no longer involved in voluntary work. Probably more significantly it authenticates the sense that the church increasingly is just 'no more'! This is very costly, especially when one considers the new role of the voluntary sector in local government in terms of the Voluntary Sector Compacts, community planning, Youth and Children's Partnerships, etc. (see above).

In researching for this chapter the membership of a South Wales County Voluntary Council was examined. It had 140 members on its website (there would be others who have asked their details not to be published), of which just one was a church and three were Christian organisations. If the churches involved with voluntary work within that local authority joined the CVC then the largest membership category would be churches and we would have to be taken seriously by local government. Ironically of course, as a very senior local government official reflected to me recently, these bodies used to be led by churches.

Having stressed the importance of engaging with your CVC for reasons of political representation, it is of course essential to recognise the significance of the key practical services which they provide. Among other things CVCs:

- Provide an important source of information about funding streams from the local authority and beyond.
- Alert the voluntary sector to changes in local government policy.
- Provide numerous training opportunities.
- Provide relationship building/partnership opportunities beyond the church.

CVC websites

Details of Wales' County Voluntary Councils can be found on the web (see below). Some of the sites are well worth a visit. If there is no website listed for your CVC then do visit another site. Much of the information provided is useful across Wales. Also bear in mind that at the time of writing more and more CVCs are developing websites so by the time you read this your CVC may actually have a site.

A list of councils can be found on Wales on the Web: www.walesontheweb.org/cayw/guides/en/51

Joining your CVC

In the case of some CVCs there is a membership fee although in some cases all that is required is an e-mail!

The Wales Council for Voluntary Action

Whilst the local voice of the voluntary sector is located in the CVC, the national voice is articulated through the Wales Council for Voluntary Action (WCVA). The primary need is for local projects to join their CVC, where otherwise they have no representation, rather than the WCVA where they indirectly have an interface since Gweini is a WCVA member. Having said this, however, the more Christian voluntary sector projects that are members of the WCVA the better. If you are a national organisation or a large project then you should certainly consider membership.

Even if you decide not to join then do remember that you can always visit the WCVA websites, which are very helpful, and you can also apply for their funding streams:

The WCVA websites

General Site: The general site includes all manner of information about the voluntary sector in Wales, policy developments and funding streams (see below). Check it out!

www.wcva.org.uk

OBJECTIVE 1 SITE: The WCVA has also developed a special website, as mentioned in the previous chapter on Objective 1 and the voluntary sector. Again, if you live in an Objective 1 area, check it out!

www.wcva.org.uk/europe

The WCVA is also significant for administering a number of national funding streams. These include:

- Traws Cymru - Across Wales
- Volunteering in Wales Fund
- Balchder Bro - safeguarding and celebrating local heritage
- Community building grants scheme
- Enfys
- Local mental health grants
- Millennium volunteers
- Social Risk Fund
- You and your community

Conclusion

In conclusion, it is the recommendation of this section that church/Christian voluntary sector projects make it a priority to join their CVC, to

- raise the profile of the Christian voluntary sector within the locality
- impact the development of local authority policy, and
- access local funding streams.

This chapter would also encourage you to at least make use of the WCVA websites and funding streams. If you are a national organisation or are involved with large projects then do consider WCVA membership.

Chapter 13: Partner Three: The National Assembly for Wales

The National Assembly invests a very significant amount of money directly and indirectly in the voluntary sector. It is, as such, a very significant partner for the Christian voluntary sector.

At the time of writing there is no comprehensive list of Assembly grants for the voluntary sector. This chapter approaches Assembly funding streams through two gateways provided by the National Assembly website:

- The Social Disadvantage pages
- The Voluntary Sector pages

In considering each in turn, the chapter will pay special attention to the community regeneration strategy at the heart of the Assembly's social inclusion policy, *Communities First*.

Social disadvantage

As one of the National Assembly's three crosscutting themes, tackling social disadvantage is given special attention by the National Assembly through the **Community Purpose Fund** which over 2001-2004 is worth £83 million. The main project that the fund supports is Communities First.

Communities First

Communities First has been much celebrated. There are great hopes that its unique approach of involving the local communities from the poorest parts of Wales (88 separate communities involving 119 local authority wards) in planning and initiating their own regeneration, in a long -term programme of at least ten years, will be extremely successful. There has been a real air of expectancy that it will define best practice that other nations will follow.

The great fanfare of trumpets that announced the launch of Communities First, celebrating its place at the cornerstone of National Assembly social inclusion policy, can seem somewhat misplaced when one confronts the hard facts of the situation. £80 million sounds like a lot of money, but split between 88 communities over three years it only amounts to a few hundred thousand per community per year. The limitations of Communities First money, however, should not blind us to the strategic significance of this innovative process.

In truth Communities First money is really about investing in the creation of a state-of-the-art 'community development' framework. Such a framework, it is hoped, will be very well positioned to access monies from other sources. Seen apart from this longer-term agenda, the concentration on civic capacity building can give the impression that Communities First is more concerned with 'process', the means, than the end. This preoccupation with the means, however, is for the sake of the end, i.e. enabling communities to access the funding that will then address the more basic socio-economic problems.

In the current context Communities First is arguably a pump-priming device developed by the National Assembly to enable local communities to access Objectives 1, 2 and 3 and other monies for social projects. The aspiration is clearly that Communities First will become a means whereby the poorest communities can access very much more than approximately £800,000 every three years.

Local partnerships

Central to the Communities First's objective of developing civic capacity is the Local Partnership established on the basis of:

1. Community representatives
2. Statutory sector representatives
3. Voluntary and business representatives

In other words, this is a form of the three-thirds principle. Interestingly the Assembly explicitly includes faith groups in its definition of 'community representatives'.

Engaging with Communities First

Communities First presents the Christian voluntary sector with a need to engage with the broader voluntary sector. While money will ultimately be allocated to specific projects, a great deal of time will be devoted to developing civic capacity through generating plans and partnering with other bodies and other individuals. This is a great challenge to Christian welfare providers who would rather live in a Christian cosmos and only engage with the world at the point-of-service delivery to the homeless person, the parent and toddler, etc.

If we are to access government monies at a time when **partnership** is everything, then we must engage with partnerships. There can be no doubt that in a politically correct age this calls for great wisdom and circumspection. Equally, however, there can be no doubt that engaging with partnerships gives us a greater interface with the world through which to project our salt and light. It is not only service receivers that are in need!

Check the website and find out whether you live in

a Communities First area. Consider:

- Engaging with your local Communities First consultation process.

- Seeking membership of the Communities First Partnership. This will obviously depend upon whether membership has already been determined. If membership has already been determined this could be difficult but if membership decisions were made without the involvement of faith communities or the faith communities voluntary sector then you might want to suggest that this is an oversight that needs to be corrected with the appropriate amendment of the Partnership.

- Establishing what is required for your project to benefit from Communities First funding.

Contact the National Assembly Communities First Unit to discover the state of play with your Communities First Partnership and get involved. If you do not live in a Communities First area but provide a service in a neighbouring community accessed by people from within the Communities First area then you may be able to benefit from the Communities First process.

For further information contact:

THE COMMUNITIES FIRST UNIT
Cathays Park
Cardiff
CF10 3NQ

Tel: (029) 20823784
Fax: (029) 20825136

e-mail: communities.first@wales.gsi.gov.uk

For information about Communities First on the National Assembly Web Site visit:
http://www.wales.gov.uk/themessocialdeprivation/content/comfirsthome_e.htm

For the National Assembly's Communities First Guidance visit:
http://www.wales.gov.uk/themessocialdeprivation/content/

Engaging with the Communities First Trust Fund

The National Assembly has now launched the Communities First Trust Fund. This will be attractive for many church and para-church projects because of its relative simplicity. Individual projects can make individual bids without the level of partnership commitment central to the thrust of the mainstream Communities First process.

The Communities First Trust Fund is worth £9 million over a three-year period and covers 139 wards and sub-wards. Each ward and sub-ward is allocated £20,000 per financial year. The aspiration of the fund is that rather than giving out £20,000 to one project in each area per year, smaller grants should be made to a number of projects in the area which corporately add up to £20,000.

A WCVA Bulletin in 2002 defined the Communities First Trust Fund in the following terms: 'The Welsh Assembly Government's Communities First Trust Fund is a new grants scheme targeted at the most disadvantaged communities in Wales. The fund is managed by the Communities First Support Network on behalf of the Welsh Assembly Government and administered by WCVA.

"Small grants are available for groups in Communities First areas for any type of activity that involves local people through small community-led organisations. The Fund is aimed at supporting activities that provide economic, environmental, social or cultural benefit for people. Further details are available from the Communities First Helpline on 0800 587 8898 or email enquiries@communitiesfirst.info".[18] Send them an e-mail and ask for a fund application pack.

Voluntary sector grants

We now turn to the grants laid out under the heading voluntary sector. These are:

- Civic Initiatives (Heritage) Grants
- Grants to Welsh Archaeological Trusts
- Combating Drug and Alcohol Misuse
- Grants to National Voluntary Youth Organisations
- Support for School Governor Training Activities
- Environment Wales
- Environmental Development Fund
- Health Promotion Voluntary Grant Scheme
- Home Improvement/Care & Repair Agencies
- Prevention and Alleviation of Homelessness and Rooflessness
- Promotion of Education and Training and of Good Practice in the Management of Social Housing
- Sustainable Communities Programme
- Grants for Voluntary Organisations Operating in the Social Care Sector (on an All-Wales basis)
- Grants for Voluntary Organisations Operating in the Social Care Sector (on a local basis)
- Local Voluntary Services Scheme Support for Voluntary Intermediary Services Volunteering in Wales Fund
- Local Regeneration Fund European Funding.

Chapter 14: Partner Four: The Welsh European Funding Office

There are a series of government bodies which, while accountable to the Assembly, enjoy a significant degree of autonomy. These are called Assembly Sponsored Public Bodies (ASPBs). There are a number of ASPBs with whom the Christian voluntary sector can partner, including ELWa and the WDA. Given constraints of space, however, we will just focus on one ASPB, the Welsh European Funding Office.

During the period 2000-2006 Wales has been and is receiving substantial structural funding from the European Union (Objective 1 alone involves an EU investment of £1.61billion). The body that has been established to allocate European Structural Funds in Wales is the Welsh European Funding Office. The funds are distributed through three programmes, four Community Initiatives and a Rural Development Plan. In what follows we will concentrate on the three programmes and especially the most significant programme, Objective 1.

General principles of the European Structural Funds

Before moving to consider the different schemes in detail, however, it is important to make some general introductory comments:

Eligibility

European Structural Funds can be sought by any organisation (individuals are not eligible) that are:

- Public bodies
- Education establishments
- Training organisations
- Voluntary organisations
- Community groups
- Farmers and producing groups[19]

Match funding

European monies are only allocated on the basis that they can be matched by investments from elsewhere. The average match funding ratio for Objective 1 is 50% (although it can vary from 30% to 70%), so for every £1 million from Europe, Wales must provide £1 million. If Wales fails to provide the match-funding then the funding will not be forthcoming. Having said this, however, the prospect of a significant investment is very good at drawing in other investments. There are actually many ways of obtaining match funding (see chapter 9).[20]

Cross-cutting themes

All European programmes uphold three 'cross-cutting themes' to which applicants must demonstrate commitment. Whilst not all funding criteria specifically engage with the cross-cutting themes set out below, all monies must at least be spent in a manner that is consistent with the broad national commitment to:

- Equal opportunities
- The information society
- Environmental sustainability[21]

Objective 1

"Objective 1 for West Wales and the Valleys aims to tackle the extreme economic deprivation that has been experienced across these areas through building sustainable communities, increasing skills levels, developing employment opportunities and a strong business sector."[22]

Objective 1 is designed to address the economically most backward parts of the EU. Qualification depends on the average GDP per head being less than 75% of the EU average. West Wales has an average GDP per head of 73%, whilst the valleys have an average GDP per head of 74%. The overall average of West Wales and the Valleys is 73%, hence the region's qualification for Objective 1.[23]

So how large is West Wales and the Valleys? Does your locality fall within it? The region is defined by the boundaries of 15 out of Wales' 22 local authorities:

WEST WALES	THE VALLEYS
Denbighshire	Swansea
Conwy	Neath Port Talbot
Anglesey	Bridgend
Gwynedd	Rhondda Cynon Taff
Ceredigion	Merthyr Tydfil
Pembrokeshire	Torfaen
Carmarthenshire	Blaenau Gwent
	Caerphilly

West Wales and the Valleys have been awarded £1.16 billion Objective 1 money between 2000-2006, which when match funded will augment to £2.3 billion.[24] This is a huge investment of money especially when you consider it is for just a part of Wales.

There are two criteria hurdles over which one must pass in order to establish the kind of project that you can bid for.

The **Single Programme Document** (SPD) lays out the full breadth of criteria which have been deemed acceptable bases against which one can bid. The Single Programme Documents can be accessed from the WEFO website.

In order to demonstrate the relevance of the broad funding criteria to the kind of projects in which the Christian voluntary sector is or could become engaged, the following box lists the SPD priorities.

Single Programme Document: Objective 1 Priorities and Measures:

Priority 1 - Expanding and developing the small and medium sized enterprise (SME) base
Priority 2 - Developing innovation and the knowledge based economy
Priority 3 - Community economic regeneration
Priority 4 - Developing people
Priority 5 - Rural development

In order to embed the funding process in the different communities of the Objective 1 area, the SPD is given a sharper local focus by *Local Action Plans*. These plans are developed by bodies convened by local authorities and formed on the basis of the three-thirds principle called Local Partnerships. If a church in, for example, Ceredigion wants to make a bid it must do so in deference to the narrower criteria laid out in the Local Action Plan rather than the broader criteria in the Single Programme Document.

As well as Local Authority Partnership Action Plans there are also **Regional Partnership Action Plans** established on the same basis and for the same purpose as local plans in all respects, apart from the fact that they serve projects based within four local authorities or more. Obviously these will not be relevant to individual church projects although they could be relevant to para-church regional/national projects. At the time of writing there are 10 Regional Partnerships, each of which is defined in terms of a particular issue area:

> In this short chapter it is not possible to provide an exhaustive investigation of all the local and regional plans. There is no substitute for getting hold of the SPD, and more importantly your Local Action Plan, and reading the relevant priorities and measures in full.
>
> The plans of all the local authority and regional partnerships and contact details are listed in the Wales Council for Voluntary Action's excellent EU funding site in their VSU Library. www.wcva.org.uk/europe

Objective 2 and Transitional Programmes

"Objective 2 aims to improve identified areas across Wales that have been affected by industrial and rural decline and tackle the social and economic deprivation through developing sustainable communities, increasing employment opportunities and promoting economic diversity."[25]

The Objective 2 and Transitional geography is more difficult to describe than that of either Objective 1 or 3 because it relates to smaller areas defined in terms of wards rather then entire local authorities. These wards fall in six out of the seven Welsh local authorities that are not in the Objective 1 area. Specifically Objective 2 areas include 80 wards in Powys, 10 wards in Cardiff and 9 wards in Newport. The transitional areas, meanwhile (those that benefited from either Objective 2 or Objective 5b support in the funding round 1994 -1999 but which were not included in the Objective 2 area for the current 2000-2006 round) include 8 wards in Cardiff, 14 wards in Powys, 31 wards in Monmouthshire, 4 wards in Wrexham and 11 wards in the Vale of Glamorgan.[26]

The total Objective 2 programme is worth £128 million and comprises £51.8 million of EU money with £76.2 million of match funding. The Transitional programme is worth a total of £64.1 million, comprising £24.8 million with match funding of £39.3 million. This means that the total Objective2/ Transitional programme is worth £192.1 million.[27]

As in the case of Objective 1, the Objective 2 and Transitional Programme has a Single Programme Document. Similarly, although the boundaries of Objective 2 do not result in its covering the whole of any local authority, each relevant local authority nonetheless convenes a Local Partnership to develop a Local Action Plan for the wards in its area on the basis of the three-thirds principle. There are thus six Local Partnerships and Action Plans.

Again, as in the case of Objective 1, there is a facility for projects spanning four or more local authorities. Unlike Objective 1, however, where there are ten regional partnerships covering different specialist areas, in the case of the Objective 2 and Transitional Programme, there is just one Regional Partnership and Action Plan.

Given the constraints of space and the diversity of six plans, this chapter seeks to merely provide a taster of the opportunities presented by Objective 2 and Transitional money through a list of the Single Programme Document Priorities and Measures headings:

Priority 1 -	Developing competitive and sustainable SMEs
Priority 2 -	Sustainable rural development
Priority 3 -	Urban community development
Priority 4 -	Technical assistance

Objective 3

"Objective 3 in East Wales aims to support economic growth of the region by contributing to the sustainable development of a competitive and knowledge based economy and through promoting equal access to training, education and employment opportunities so that people can fulfil their potential."[28]

Objective 3 applies to that part of Wales not covered by the West Wales and the Valleys: the nation's remaining seven local authority areas, namely Cardiff, the Vale of Glamorgan, Newport, Monmouthshire, Powys, Flintshire and Wrexham. The amount of European money available is considerably less than that in the Objective 1 area because it has a higher GDP per head of population than the 75% of the European average or below required by Objective 1. Having said this, the amount of money available is nonetheless significant.

Objective 3 money is worth £198 million, comprising £82.5 million of EU money, with the remaining £115.6 coming from match funding. Of this, £101 million should come from the public sector while the remaining £14.6 million comes from the private sector.[29]

Operational programme and relevant plan

Objective 3's single programme document equivalent is called the 'Operational Programme'. Again it will be important to study this, but again its priorities will be given different emphases by the Local Partnerships and the Local Partnership Plans. As in the case of Objective 1 and 2, the local authority and regional approach to plans is adopted. There are seven Local Partnership Plans, one for each local authority and one regional plan for the whole East Wales area. To obtain copies of your Local Plan, and the contact details for your Local Partnership, contact your local authority.

As in the case of Objective 1 and 2, in the interests of providing a window on the kind of funding opportunities presented by Objective 3 we provide the headings for its priorities and measures.

Objective 3 Priorities and Measures:

Priority 1 - Promoting active labour policies to reduce unemployment
Priority 2 - Equal opportunities for all and promoting social inclusion
Priority 3 - Lifelong learning
Priority 4 - Promoting business competitiveness
Priority 5 - Promoting gender equality in the labour market

To find out more about the community initiatives visit the Wales European Funding Office website.

Social Risk Fund

For many church projects a more appropriate way of accessing Objective 1 and 3 will be through the Social Risk Fund. The Wales Council for Voluntary Action has been given the responsibility of allocating small grants from Objective 1 and 3 to voluntary projects across the nation. The benefit of this money is that obtaining it is an infinitely less complex process than putting in a conventional bid. The downside is that grants are limited to £10,000. Nevertheless this is a significant amount of money! The money is targeted at projects that combat social exclusion and contribute to local regeneration.

Key Contact Details

Emyr Williams
Social Risk Fund Advisor

Tel 01492 539808

Email: ewilliams@wcva.org.uk

THE WELSH EUROPEAN FUNDING OFFICE (WEFO)

The Old Primary School
Machynlleth
SY20 8PE
Tel: (01654) 704900
Fax: (01654 704909

Cynon Business Park
Mountain Ash
CF45 4ER
Tel: (01443) 471100
Fax: (01443) 471120

Cathays Park
Cardiff
CF10 3NQ
Tel: (029) 2082 5111
Fax: (029) 2082 379

www.wefo.wales.gov.uk

Of great significant for the voluntary sector, readers should be aware that the Wales Council for Voluntary Action has established a European Funding Help Desk which can receive calls from 8am - 6pm Monday to Friday. They have also created a website dealing with Objective 1 applications only. Created specifically for the voluntary sector there is a real sense in which this is more useful than the WEFO site.

Wales Council for Voluntary Action (WCVA)

EU Funding Helpdesk: 0870 607 1666

Objective 1 website: www.wcva.org.uk/europe

Email: help@wcva.org.uk

CONCLUSION
THE CHURCH THAT ORDAINED WAITERS

By Elfed Godding

Seven elders laid hands on me when I was ordained and inducted into my first pastorate. Twenty-three years later I still relive the excitement of being set apart as a minister of the gospel and that should be no surprise since it is both a biblical and traditional practice for releasing men and women into the pastoral ministry. Surprisingly though, for some of us it was also standard biblical practice to ordain 'social servers' in exactly the same way!

When the early church in Acts 6 faced a growth crisis it was faced with a stark choice. Should they become a safe 'fortress' or a risky 'frontier' church? So many new people had joined, bringing their social and cultural distinctives, that the leaders had to decide if they were going to build safe and secure theological walls around their existing accomplishments, or press out into their community to extend the Kingdom. Were they to monopolise Christian ministry or delegate for expansion?

As well as the increasing dynamism and multiculturalism of the many new converts the church faced the challenge of social activism. Acts 6:1 cites the "daily distribution of food". It did not take long for their faith to express itself in love, but this increased the pressure on leadership: how can we cope with serving the community and preaching the Word? Here lies the potential breaking point: do we build a fortress to protect what we have, or push the frontiers, risking the safe structures we have built?

Amazingly the solution to the crisis was not to increase the number of paid clergy. Instead they affirmed priorities. The priority ministry for the 12 was "proclaiming the Word" while the priority ministry for the Seven was "waiting on tables". Just waiting on tables would produce a social gospel. Just preaching the Word would produce a theorised gospel. They became an effective first-century church by doing both.

Ministries were willingly delegated and servants were commissioned. The apostles "laid their hands on them". Here the act we normally reserve for ordaining ministers and clergy was used to initiate the Spirit-filled ministry of the waiters.

The challenge of this book is to do just that! To ordain waiters! It is our conviction that as local churches we need to engage effectively with our community and make a difference. We cannot do this until we pray, resource and back our social servers as much as we do our ministers, evangelists and missionaries. The result in Acts 6 was rapid church growth - the church was turned inside out to turn the world upside down.

OTHER GWEINI PUBLICATIONS

Taking Our Place: Church In the Community

If you have found *The Naked Church* helpful and want to go deeper, then *Taking Our Place: Church in Community* is the book for you. First published in 2002 and then substantially revised and updated in 2004, *Taking Our Place* provides a very much more detailed (214 pages) assessment of the opportunities and challenges facing the Christian Voluntary Sector in Wales today. An important 'how to' manual for engagement, it is a 'must read' for anyone wanting to advance Christian welfare provision in their community!

It has been warmly received.

'This book will prove invaluable to any church seeking to engage with government and community.'

Janet Ryder AM (North Wales)

'*Taking Our Place* provides the churches with an invaluable and informative resource in the area of delivering faith-based welfare provision in Wales. A copy should have crossed every church leader's desk.'

Rev. Aled Edwards,Cytun Churches
National Assembly Liaison Officer

'Essential reading for all church leaders who want to take the Good News to the local communities they seek to serve.'

Gary Streeter MP

'A powerful tool in the armoury of the Welsh church, equipping it to be a grass-roots, transforming 'movement for change', ... [it] defines the great challenges and opportunities facing the Welsh and indeed wider British Christian Voluntary Sector.'

Rev. Joel Edwards,
General Director Evangelical Alliance UK

To obtain your copy contact:

GWEINI: The Council of Christian Community Work in Wales,
PO Box 601
Cardiff CF10 1YR
(029) 20232852
(Discount for members).

Gweini News

Gweini also produces a bilingual newspaper called Gweini News. To obtain a free copy of the latest edition contact the Gweini office.

Gweini website

Many other Gweini publications such as 'Gweini Members Briefing Papers' are available, together with a lot of helpful information about funding and policy development, and all the very latest news, on the Gweini website.

www.gweini.org.uk

Footnotes

1 *Encounters on the Edge* No 13, Church Army Sheffield Centre (no date).

2 'Kindness' in *New International Dictionary of New Testament Theology* vol. 2, ed. Colin Brown (Paternoster Press 1976).

3 *Taking Our Place* (Gweini, 2000).

4 There is diversity between authorities, some being more generous to the voluntary sector than others.

5 The Voluntary Sector Partnership Council, 'The Voluntary Sector and Local Authorities in Wales - 1998-99 Survey of Support for Voluntary Organisations in Wales', 3.5, p. 5. (VSPC) (01) 16. Crown Copyright.

6 National Assembly for Wales, '*Extending Entitlement: Supporting Young People in Wales: Consultation of the Draft and Guidance*', November 2001, p. 21, Annex 1. Crown Copyright.

7 In moving to consider the other local authority plans and partnerships, however, it is important to be clear about priority. In seeking to make the most of the new interfaces between the voluntary sector and local government, there can be no doubt that every church's priority must be the Community Strategy given its influence and local authorities' obligation to engage with faith communities. Similarly given the extent of our involvement, the Children and Young People's Framework must also be a priority.

8 National Assembly for Wales, '*Extending Entitlement: Supporting Young People in Wales*', 2001, Annex 1,p.21.

9 Communities Directorate Welsh Assembly Government, '*Annual Report on Social Inclusion in Wales*', 2002, 5.10. Crown Copyright.

10 National Assembly for Wales, '*Improving Health in Wales - A Plan for the NHS* ', July 2001, pp. 8-9. Crown Copyright. More significant than the development of the Local Authority Health and Wellbeing Strategy was the replacement of 5 Health Authorities with 22 Local Health Boards in April 2003, each containing two voluntary sector seats. This constitutes an important salt and light challenge/opportunity for the Christian voluntary sector.

11 Ibid, p. 23, para 4.3.

12 This is seen in both the English and Welsh guidance.

Ibid, p. 18, para 3.6. '*Preparing Community Strategies*', DTLR (December 2000). Crown copyright.

13 '*Faith and Communities*', p. 34.

14 The Welsh Office and Welsh Council for Voluntary Action, *The Voluntary Sector Compact'*, 1998, p. 10.

15 Welsh Office and Wales Council for Voluntary Action, '*Compact between the Government and the Voluntary Sector in Wales'*, November 1998.

16 These groups go by different names in different local authorities.

17 For further reading on sustainable development see: Daniel Boucher, '*Sustainable Development in Wales: How Should the Christian Community Respond?*', Gweini, 2000; Daniel Boucher, '*Wales: A Community of Communities*', Gweini, April 2000.

18 Wales Council for Voluntary Action, E-Briefing, 15 April 2002.

19 Gareth Jones, '*A Guide to European Funding in Wales 2000-2006*', New Edition May 2002, Institute of Welsh Affairs, May 2002, p. 59.

20 Ibid., p. 5.

21 Ibid., pp. 16, 30 & 35.

22 National Assembly website http://www.wales.gov.uk/themesvoluntarysector/grantsguide-e.htm. Crown copyright.

23 Gareth Jones, '*A Guide to European Funding in Wales 2000-2006*', New Edition May 2002, Institute of Welsh Affairs, May 2002, p. 15.

24 Ibid.

25 National Assembly website http://www.wales.gov.uk/themesvoluntarysector/grantsguide-e.htm. Crown copyright.

26 Gareth Jones, '*A Guide to European Funding in Wales 2000-2006*', p. 28.

27 Ibid, p. 29.

28 National Assembly website http://www.wales.gov.uk/themesvoluntarysector/grantsguide-e.htm.Crown copyright.

29 Gareth Jones, '*A Guide to European Funding in Wales 2000-2006*', p. 34.